To
Robin,

Love lasts
forever...
before and after
the people in it.

always and forever
Love,
Steve

Happy St. Valentine's Day 1994

COWBOY LOVE
POETRY

♥

Girl of the brown eyes, the clear eyes, the dear eyes,
    What would you do for me, love,
    For me, love, for me, love?
I'd follow you the long trail thro',
My fears for you, my tears for you,
For you, love, for you, love.

Boy of my dreams, my whole dreams, my soul dreams,
    What would you do for me, love,
    For me, love, for me, love?
I'd shelter you the long trail thro'
My care for you, my share for you,
For you, love, for you, love.

                    Robert V. Carr

COWBOY LOVE
P O E T R Y

VERSE FROM THE HEART
OF THE WEST

Compiled and edited by

**Paddy Calistro, Jack Lamb
and Jean Penn**

Foreword by

Waddie Mitchell

Design by Jeff Darnall

ANGEL CITY PRESS

ANGEL CITY PRESS, INC.
Published by Angel City Press
2210 Wilshire Boulevard, Suite 880
Santa Monica, California 90403
(310) 395-9982

First published in 1994 by Angel City Press
1 3 5 7 9 10 8 6 4 2
FIRST EDITION

Publisher's Cataloging in Publication

Cowboy love poetry : verse from the heart of the West /
compiled and edited by Paddy Calistro, Jack R. Lamb
and Jean Penn ; foreword by Waddie Mitchell.
192 p. 14 cm.
Includes bibliographical references and index.
ISBN 1-883318-45-9

1. Folk poetry, American. 2. Cowboys—Poetry.
3. Love poetry, American. I. Calistro, Paddy.
II. Lamb, Jack R.   III. Penn, Jean.

PS477.5.C67C69 1994   811'.044'08352636

Library of Congress Card Catalog Number: 93-74618
Printed in the United States of America

To

Ellen Hoffs

and

Scott McAuley

CONTENTS

FOREWORD

Not too many years ago, before "Cowboy Poetry" was discovered by folklorists like Hal Cannon who recognized its worth, we cowboy poets had very little to do. We just wrote our little ditties for the cowboys, ranchers and country folk of the "inner circle" of our lifestyle.

In the last decade, though, that has changed. Cowboy poetry is finding its own way into the publishing and entertainment arena. The interest has been phenomenal. Yet, until now, no one has focussed on the sentimental love poetry of the genre.

Maybe that's because love is a subject rarely touched on by the cowboy writers. After all, we typically write about what we know. The lifestyle does not abound with the opportunities afforded those living in or around females all the time. Since insight is derived from experience, the cowboy is often at a disadvantage when it comes to love. When love happens into his life, he might not know how to handle it. Or how to express it. He wants it. He dreams about it. But he doesn't always understand it. A young cowboy, who might depend on the experiences of an older cowboy for help on the subject of love, might gain a distorted view as in the case of "Wild Horse Charlie," a classic poem from the early part of this century:

> We were gatherin' remnant yearlins
> On the Cross Bar Lazy B
> When the foreman, Wild Horse Charlie,
> Lit his pipe and said to me:
>
> "Now I ain't a-claimin' that a female
> May not be the proper dope,
> But, as for me, I'm more contented
> With my bronco and my rope.
>
> "An' I ain't a-knowin' nothin'
> Of the species, pard, ya see,

Cuz one dad-burned adventure
Was a-plenty 'nuf for me.

"Said she taught the school at Dobie
An' I will state in comment wide
That a better lookin' critter
Never crossed the Great Divide.

"I was losin' all my senses
An' went trailin' her until
I finally popped the question
An' she answered with 'I will!'

"We had it figger'd nicely.
We would meet in Santa Fe
At the courthouse to be married
On the twenty-third of May.

"Well, I arrived there for the weddin'
Right on schedule, and I'll say
There's never been as many punchers
Ever seen in Santa Fe.

"They was hangin' 'round the courthouse
An' I figger'd they was wise
To our secret little nuptials
An' aimed to give us a surprise.

"So I kept a-waitin', waitin' patient
For my blushin' little bride
When the sheriff got a message
An' he called us all inside.

"It was just a little message
From some town in Illinois,
Readin' 'On my way to Boston,
Give my best to all the boys.'

"An' as the plot developed
We learned that scheming little bait
Was engaged to all the punchers
She could locate in the state.

"An' we all had give her money,
A hundred bucks a school,
Jest to learn a woman's heartless
An' a puncher's jest a fool!

"Well, I ambled home in sadness
An' I'm sayin' straight to you
That I'm all cut-up on women
Which is meanin' that I'm through."

"But most of them is noble,
Good an' true," I weakly said,
But the foreman, Wild Horse Charlie,
Never spoke nor turned his head.

With everything a cowboy had going against him, if he
was lucky enough to land himself a wife, then the reality of
what he could offer would set in. I touched on that subject after
one lean Christmas. I call it, "There's Nothin' Like Nothin'":

'Twas their fourteenth Christmas together.
'Cept for the kids, didn't have much to show
For the life he'd spent ridin' for cattle
And he was feeling especially low.

For if ever a wife was obliging,
If ever a woman endured,
Then surely she was at the top of the list
And a gift from her man was deserved.

But he'd been kick'd and was somewhat lame
And a trip to the doc don't come free

And extra money from startin' colts
Don't get made with a busted-up knee.

Oh, the kids would get by with the trinkets they'd buy
From hair ropes he had traded in town,
And peanut brittle gold from ma's recipe old
Would help weight little Christmas socks down.

But for her there was no silver package
And that surely weighed heavy on he,
For this year especially he wanted
To have something for her 'neath the tree.

That night he said, "Dear, I've a question.
Would you come here by me and sit down.
Do you think I am wrong punchin' cattle?
And should I find me a good job in town?

"One that would make our life easier
With good pay and benefits too!
With two weeks vacation, a company car,
And a retirement plan when I'm through."

She smiled and put her arm 'round him
Said, "You've work'd yourself up in a stew.
There's nothin' like nothin' for Christmas,
When I get to share it with you.

"Cuz you are the man that I wanted and chose,
To live with 'til our days here are gone.
And one of the things that attracted me most
Was the lifestyle and ranches we'd live on.

"And that is as much a part of us now
As anything else is for sure.
And to move us to town and lose what we have
Would be nothing but misery pure.

So don't worry 'bout presents for Christmas,
And listen up he-buckaroo,
There's nothin' like nothin' for Christmas,
When I know it's comin' from you.

Whether a cowboy is writing about a romance gone wrong or a long-lasting love, the words don't come easy. As many poems as I've written, and as many emotions as I've tried to express, writing about love is still the most awkward. Sometimes I just get tongue-tied and decide to steer clear of the topic. That seems to be a common quirk among cowpunchers, and that's surely one of the reasons the collection of poems in this book is so unusual. Classic cowboy love poems are a rare commodity. But when the words did come, they were honest, heartfelt and well thought out. Cowboys past and present haven't had all the distractions of city life; they had time out on the range to dig deep into their souls and try to understand what they were feeling.

Compared to today's shock-factor sensationalism towards love themes, the almost Victorian innocence of the cowboy's approach to the subject may seem outdated. Although contemporary poets come closer to touchin' on sex, on the whole, there is still a more innocent romance implied. I think half of romance is the fantasy involved with it. If we lose the mental cloak and have only blatant realities, then I believe we are in serious jeopardy of losing the images of romance so essential to happiness.

I find Cowboy Love Poetry to be charming. I believe it will become a classic read aloud for years to come by those courting new found loves as well as those courting their love of many years. To those of you lucky enough to find this book, I say to you, enjoy it. It sure works for me!

—*Waddie Mitchell*
Elko, Nevada

INTRODUCTION

Lonesome? Well, I guess so!
This place is mighty blue:
The silence of the empty rooms
Jes' palpitates with — you."

–anonymous

Romantic, soulful love poetry? By cowboys? Plenty of friends, and not just city slickers, were surprised that we were publishing such a book. Legend has it that cowboys are real stoics, wild and wooly untamables of uncomplicated thoughts and few syllables. Many of our city friends didn't even know that working cowboys have been spouting poetry and making up verses since the first cattle drives over a century ago, and are still doing so today at gatherings in Elko, Nevada and other spots throughout the west.

Not all the doubters were dudes. Cowboys and cowgirls themselves were surprised at the gold mine of love poetry that exists, spanning a century of Western literary culture. A personal chronicle of the working cowboys' life, most cowboy poetry tells us how they work and play, how they relish the range and herd and brand the cattle, and their thoughts about their lives and chores.

Rarer are the love poems, but they're as vividly descriptive as the poets' other works. And you can kiss goodbye the stereotypical "macho" cowboy who handles emotions as stoically as he handles an Injun attack. America's most romanticized heroes were and are hopeless sentimentalists. Their poetry reveals life's rich pageant of emotions — from bewilderment to anguish and joy — as they, sometimes unwillingly, open up their arms and hearts to the opposite sex. When they fall, it is with a mighty, momentous and often humorous thud. Whether told with levity or sorrow, their verses of love are as important to the whole picture of the American frontier people as odes to the land, horses, freedom and the sky above.

Cowboy poetry had its beginnings after the Civil War. During three- to six-month long cattle drives from the rangelands of Texas and Kansas to shipping points in the plains of mid-America, cowboys entertained each other around the campfire at night by swapping verses they had learned or written. Sometimes they were poems clipped from western newspapers, fitted to a popular tune. Poems passed from one cowboy to another and, as performers saw fit, they added verses and changed words. But cowpokes were shy about sharing their words of love, often keeping them hidden in their saddlebags and maybe reciting them to their beloveds.

The cowboy's love poetry, from the start, was as unique as his other verses, and often displayed the same self-deprecating or boastful humor. It seems that cowboys — who didn't earn much money or offer much stability — were much luckier with their horses than with the ladies. They lived in a man's world most the time, staying in cow camps for months at a time, eating out of chuckwagons, rarely coming back to the home ranch or town. As 87-year-old cowboy poet Slim Kite remembers, "You might see a girl once in a while, but it might be six months before you found out who she was."

When a swell-looking woman happened by — say the foreman's niece from Boston or a new schoolmarm with rosy cheeks and twinkling eyes — the smitten cowboys were apt to go bonkers, getting slicked every night, some even sneaking down to the creek to scrub up, situations E.A. Brininstool, among others, describes in several of his poems.

In "A Cowboy's Hopeless Love," by James Barton Adams, the lovestruck cowboy, moping around like a lost calf, cries out:

I wish to God she'd never come with them bright
    laughin' eyes, —
Had never flashed that smile that seems a sunburst
    from the skies, —
Had stayed there in her city home instead o' coming here
To visit at the ranch an' knock my heart plumb out o' gear.

In poetry about courtship, we see the cowboy in his most awkward and amusing moments, falling all over himself, oft too bashful to speak at the moment of truth. Ambivalence about love and marriage is another source of poetic inspiration. Although moral redemption through love of a good woman — one who would say "honey, I'm here for the ride," — is much celebrated, the average working cowboy's wage wasn't enough to support a family. Getting lassoed by love meant losing the freedom to roam. In "Them Heap Big Thoughts," Robert V. Carr writes, "when love rides 'cross a feller's range, he thinks thoughts of a wholesale store."

Much of the poetry reflects a "Don't Fence Me In" attitude about love, echoing the sentiment that romance is a trap designed to rob a man of his freedom. Still, as James Barton Adams writes in "A Cowboy's Worrying Love," a poem full of cranky sighs and irony, "I'm seein' it different now." And Charles "Badger" Clark in "The Tied Maverick" tells of one high-headed bronco sinner, corralled and caught, roped and tied with roses.

Such is the cowboy's special way of expressing his emotions. You'll find no hidden codes, no obscure imagery, references or buried meanings that require an English literature degree. Indeed, the verses are meant to be shared, read aloud with gusto. The images are simple, strong and memorable, just like the American cowboy.—*The Editors*

Chapter 1

THE LOVESTRUCK COWBOY

ut on the range, the cowboy didn't have many opportunities for romance. So when Cupid's arrow finally pierced a buckaroo's stolid heart, the lovestruck cowboy fell with a hard and sometimes humorous thud. So locoed by love were they, some cowpunchers even took to writing verse, penning rhymes like "It hain't no use / Fer me to try a raise a hand / When on my heart she's run her brand."

JUANITA

E.A. Brininstool

Drear are the prairies, the ranges are silent,
Mournfully whispers each soft, passing breeze.
Down in the canyon an eddying murmur
Echoes the sigh through the swaying pine trees.
Lone are the trails on the brown, dusty mesa,
Up where the gems of the star-world peep through;
Sadly the nightbird is plaintively calling —
'Nita, Juanita, I'm longing for you!

Out where the herds dot the range in the Springtime,
Out where the flowers you loved nod and sway,
Memory brings me a vision of sadness,
Brings me a dream of a once-happy day.
Over the trails you are riding beside me,
Under the canopied heavens of blue;
Smiling the love that your lips have repeated —
'Nita, Juanita, I'm longing for you!

When steals the night with its grim, dusky shadows,
As 'round the herd I am jogging along,
Your gentle face seems to lighten the darkness,
Each vagrant breeze seems to whisper a song.
Whispers a melody sweetly entrancing,
Telling me, dear, of your love ever true;
Whispers an echo that sets my heart dancing —
'Nita, Juanita, I'm longing for you!

"CUPID" ON A COW RANCH

E.A. Brininstool

A Boston gal, the foreman's niece,
Is here to spend a month er two,
An' sence she come, there ain't no peace –
The boys is locoed clean plumb through!
They buy b'iled shirts an' fancy socks,
An' try to sling on loads o' style,
An' go to town an' blow their rocks
Fer presents every little while!

I never seen sich monkey biz
On this here cattle ranch afore!
The foreman says that niece o' his
Has set the bunkhouse in a roar!
The boys they try to comb their hair,
An' slick it up with ile an' dope!
An' jes' fer plain cow hands, I swear
They're usin' up a raft o' soap!

Pink Bates is shavin' ev'ry night!
An' Shorty goes down to the crick
An' scrubs hisself till he's as white
As any dood! It makes me sick!
An' gosh! the dog they're slingin' on
When they strut out to the corral!
An' all becuz they're jes' dead-gone
On that swell-lookin' Boston gal!

I don't know how it's comin' out!
She ain't give anyone a hunch!
But you would think, to hear 'em spout,
That she's dead-stuck on all the bunch!
I don't know how she'll end the race,
But here is what I hope, by jing:
That she won't hang around this place
Until the roundup starts next Spring!

A LOCOED OUTFIT
E.A. Brininstool

The new schoolmarm on Bear Paw Creek
Has rosy cheeks an' twinklin' eyes;
She's got my round-up crew lovesick;
I never seen such locoed guys.

They want to shave now ev'ry day,
An' ile their hair an' change their clo'es.
The round-up's workin' down this way,
But they won't ride, I don't suppose.

Instid o' blowin' in their rocks
Fer silver spurs an' guns an' things,
They buy b'iled shirts an' fancy socks,
Store ties an' collars too, by jings!

I don't suppose it's nothin' strange,
'Cuz gals is scarce around these parts;
Though she's ten mile across the range,
She's sure stirred my cowpuncher's hearts.

If they go out a-huntin' strays,
Er ridin' fence, they're sure to roam
To'rds Bear Paw Creek, to ride a ways
With that there schoolmarm, goin' home.

They sure close-herd that schoolmarm gal;
They're lovers that don't shirk;
They hang around her home corral,
And do blamed little cowpunch work.

They moon around the bunkhouse door,
Plumb jealous of each other too;
I wish that gal would hike afore
She hypnotizes 'em clean through!

LOVE ON THE "BAR-X"

E.A. Brininstool

I thought I was free as the cattle
A-roamin' around on the range,
But Cupid is here givin' battle,
An' got me corralled for a change.
I'm stampeded sure by the glances
She throws from them twinklin' brown eyes,
An' jealous plumb through if she prances
Around with them other range guys.

The purtiest heifer a-herdin'
Around there in Cupid's corral
That sure is the proper-style wordin'
Describin' her truly an' well.
I never went much on this lovin';
I allus was bashful from birth,
But now to the front I am shovin',
An playin' the game all it's worth.

I'm tryin' to tame my rough manner
To fit with her Bostonese style;
She dances an' hits the pianner,
An' Lordy, she's got a swell smile!
The boys of the Bar-X start jeerin'
Whenever I go shyin' 'round
An' josh me if I go to steerin'
An' nosin' on her stompin' ground.

I wasn't quite ready to brand her;
Been browsin' around, so to say;
But when I git ready to land her,
You want to clear out o' my way!
She hain't halter-broke to my teasin';
She bucks if I go it too fur,
But I hain't seen nary a reason
Why I won't hitch double with her.

I've tackled the parson about her —
He says to corral her darned quick.
I cain't ride through life now without her;
When I think of it — gosh, I git sick!
That's her lopin' off down the coulee —
I reck'n, ol' hawss, we'll go see
If she'll double up with yours truly,
An' ride on the life-range with me!

THE COWGIRL

E.A. Brininstool

She ain't inclined to'rds lots o' things
That Eastern gals kin do up brown!
She don't wear jewelry an' rings,
Like them swell gals that lives in town.
Her cheeks are tanned an olive tint
That shows the roses hidin' there;
Her eyes are brown, and there's a hint
Of midnight in her wavin' hair.

She don't go in for fancy hats,
A wide-brimmed Stetson is her pet.
She has no use for puffs and rats,
And harem skirts would make her fret.
She wears a 'kerchief 'round her neck,
At breakin' broncs she shows her sand;
And at a round-up she's on deck,
And twirls a rope with practiced hand!

She doesn't know a thing about
Them motor cyars that buzz and whirr;
But when she goes a-ridin' out,
A tough cow-pony pleases her.
Her hands are tanned to match her cheeks,
Her smile will start your heart a-whirl,
And when she looks at you and speaks,
You love this rosy, wild cowgirl!

She never saw a tennis court,
She don't belong to any club!
But she is keen to all range sport,
And she's a peach at cookin' grub!
She couldn't win at playin' whist,
She wouldn't think that bridge was fun,
But say — the *hombre* don't exist
That beats her handlin' a six-gun!

I don't believe she'd make a hit
At them swell afternoon affairs;
She wouldn't feel at home a bit,
Them ain't the things for which she cares.
She ain't so keen as some gals is
At tryin' stunts that's new and strange,
But you kin bet she knows her biz
When she's out on the cattle range!

A COWBOY'S LOVE SONG
(anonymous)

Oh, the last steer has been branded
And the last beef has been shipped,
And I'm free to roam the prairies
That the round-up crew has stripped;
I'm free to think of Susie, –
Fairer than the stars above, –
She's the waitress at the station
And she is my turtle dove.

Chorus:
Biscuit-shootin' Susie, –
She's got us roped and tied;
Sober men or woozy
Look on her with pride.
Susie's strong and able,
And not a one gits rash
When she waits on the table
And superintends the hash.

Oh, I sometimes think I'm locoed
An' jes' fit fer herdin' sheep,
'Cause I only think of Susie
When I'm wakin' or I'm sleep.
I'm wearin' Cupid's hobbles,
An' I'm tied to Love's stake-pin,
And when my heart was branded
The irons sunk deep in.

Chorus
I take my saddle, Sundays, —
The one with inlaid flaps, —
And don my new sombrero
And my white angora chaps;
Then I take a bronc for Susie
And she leaves her pots and pans
And we figure out our future
And talk o'er our homestead plans.

Chorus

A ROMANCE OF THE RANGE

Robert V. Carr

She's been out here a-teachin' this winter now
    that's past,
An' I hear that she's a-tellin' that it's
    jes' about her last —
That she's goin' to quit the schoolroom an'
    goin' home to stay —
An' somehow I'm jes' hatin' fer to see her
    go away.
Fer us fellers think that schoolmarm is an
    angel; yes, we do —
A little blue-eyed angel, yet a woman thro'
    an' thro';
An' she treats us all so kindly, jes' the' same
    'most ev'ry day,
That somehow I'm jes' hatin' fer to see her
    go away.
She hain't never give me reasons fer to
    think I'd have a show
To win her, but I'm honest when I say I like
    her so
That I dread her time fer goin', count ev'ry
    passin' day,
'Cause I'm hatin', jes' a-hatin', fer to see her
    go away.

Well, her term is 'bout completed an', say, I
    don't think I
Have got the nerve to greet her fer to say a
    last goodby;
Seems so tough! Oh, well, I'm feelin', call it
    heartsick, if you may —
'Cause I'm hatin', jes' a-hatin', fer to see her
    go away.

LATER

Oh, say, I'm 'bout as happy as a feller wants
    to be;
Went to see her an', by glory, she jes'
    upped an' cried — you see!
An' right there I had to say it, what so long
    I've feerd to say,
An' now we've gone an fixed it so she'll
    never go away.

THEM HEAP BIG THOUGHTS

Robert V. Carr

It seems to me some passin' strange,
When Love rides 'cross a feller's range,
He thinks of thoughts a wholesale store,
Such thoughts he never thought before:
Them heap big thoughts, as Injuns say,
Of life an' death an' music gay,
An' flags an' crowds an' flashin' things,
An' then sometimes he backward springs
To thoughts o' mountains big an' high,
Where giants set an' watch the sky
At sunset grand an' great an' still,
An' all the world seems dreamin' 'til
He looks around to hear this call:
"You're jes' in love, my boy, that's all."

LOVE LYRICS OF A COWBOY
Robert V. Carr

It hain't no use fer me to say
There's others with a style an' way
That beats hers to a fare-you-well,
Fer, on the square, I'm here to tell
I jes' can't even start to see
But what she's perfect as kin be.
Fer any fault I finds excuse —
I'll tell you, pard, it hain't no use
Fer me to try to raise a hand,
When on my heart she's run her brand.

The bunk-house ain't the same to me;
The bunch jes' makes me weary — Gee!
I never knew they was so coarse —
I warps my face to try to force
A smile at each old gag they spring;
Fer I'd heap ruther hear her sing
"Sweet Adeline," or softly play
The "Dream o' Heaven" that-a-way.
Besides this place, most anywhere
I'd ruther be — so she was there.

She called me "dear," an' do you know,
My heart jes' skipped a beat, an' tho'
I'm hard to feaze, I'm free to yip
My reason nearly lost its grip.
She called me "dear," jes' sweet,
An' lookin' down an' speakin' low
An' if I had ten lives to live,
With everything the world could give
I'd shake 'em all without one fear,
If 'fore I'd go she'd call me "dear."

You wonders why I slicks up so
On Sundays, when I gits to go
To see her — well, I'm free to say,
She's like religion that-a-way.
Jes sort o' like some holy thing,
As clean as young grass in the spring.
An' so before I rides to her
I looks my best from hat to spur —
But even then I hain't no right
To think I look good in her sight.

If she should pass me up — say, boy,
You jes' put hobbles on your joy;
First thing you know, you gits so gay
Your luck stampedes and gits away.
An' don't you even start a guess

That you've a cinch on happiness;
Fer few e'er reach the Promised Land
If they starts headed by a band.
Ride slow an' quiet, humble, too,
Or Fate will slap its brand on you.

The old range sleeps, there hain't a stir.
Less it's a night-hawk's sudden whir,
Or cottonwoods a-whisperin' while
The red moon smiles a lovin' smile.
An' there I set an' hold her hand
So glad I jes' can't understand
The reason of it all, or see
Why all the world looks good to me;
Or why I sees in it heap more
Of beauty than I seen before.

Fool talk, perhaps, but it jes' seems
We're ridin' through a range o' dreams;
Where medder larks the year 'round sing,
An' it's jes' one eternal spring.
An' time — why time is gone — by gee!
There's no such thing as time to me
Until she says, "Here, boy, you know
You simply jes' have got to go;
It's nearly twelve." I rides away,
"Dog-gone a clock!" is what I say.

THAT THERE GIRL
Robert V. Carr

It's that there girl 'most all the time,
Fer workin' I hain't worth a dime;
An' jes' can't turn around or stir
Without some foolish thought o' her.
Can scarcely sleep or eat my chuck —
Dog-gone the luck! I guess I'm stuck!

REAL AFFECTION

Robert V. Carr

If I could say the words I think,
My tongue with overwork would bust;
I'd make old Shakespeare rise an' say:
"What varlot now disturbs my dust!"
If I would do the things which I
Am simply achin' to perform,
I'd rope the lightnin' an' I'd jerk
The terror from the blindin' storm.

I'd use a comet fer a bronk,
An' ride him stuck-up like an' proud;
My spurs would be a pair of stars,
My blanket jes' a fleecy cloud.
I'd roundup all the planets an'
I'd do it sudden, sure an' soon,
An' then I'd set back ca'm an' watch
Them mill around the helpless moon.

I'd do all this an' maybe more,
Pervidin' that I thought it would
To this here busted heart of mine
Do any sort of passin' good.
I'd do it all an' take a chance
To hold the trail thro' Afterwhile,
If she would throw me jes' one word
An' tie it up with one sweet smile.

A NEVADA COWPUNCHER TO HIS BELOVED
(anonymous)

Lonesome? Well, I guess so!
This place is mighty blue;
The silence of the empty rooms
Jes' palpitates with — you.

The day has lost its beauty,
The sun's a-shinin' pale;
I'll round up my belongin's
An' I guess I'll hit the trail.

Out there in the sage-brush
A-harkin' to the "Coo-oo"
Of the wild dove in his matin'
I can think alone of you.

Perhaps a gaunt coyote
Will go a-lopin' by
An' linger on the mountain ridge
An' cock his wary eye.

An' when the evenin' settles,
A-waitin' for the dawn
Perhaps I'll hear the ground owl:
"She's gone — she's gone — she's gone!"

A COWBOY'S WORRYING LOVE

James Barton Adams

I ust to read in the novel books 'bout fellers that
    got the prod
From an arrer shot from his hidin' place by the
    hand o' the Cupid god,
An' I'd laugh at the cussed chumps they was a-
    wastin' their breath in sighs
An' goin' around with a locoed look a-campin' inside
    their eyes.
I've read o' the gals that broke 'em up a-sailin' in
    airy flight
On angel pinions above their beds as they dreampt o'
    the same at night,
An' a sort o' disgusted frown'd bunch the wrinkles
    acrost my brow,
An' I'd call 'em a lot o' sissy boys — but I'm seein' it
    different now.

I got the jab in my rough ol' heart, an' I got it a-
    plenty, too,
A center shot from a pair o' eyes of the winninest
    sort o' blue,
An' I ride the ranges a-sighin' sighs, as cranky as a
    locoed steer —
A durned heap worse than the novel blokes that the
    narrative gals'd queer.
Just hain't no energy left no mo', go 'round like a
    orphant calf
A-thinkin' about that sagehen's eyes that give me
    the Cupid gaff,
An' I'm all skeered up when I hit the thought some
    other rider might
Cut in ahead on a faster hoss an' rope her afore
    my sight.

There ain't a heifer that ever run in the feminine
    beauty herd
Could switch a tail on the whole durned range 'long-
    side o' that little bird;
A figger plump as a prairy dog's that's feedin' on
    new spring grass,
An' as purty a face as was ever flashed in front of a
    lookin' glass.
She's got a smile that'd raise the steam in the icyist
    sort o' heart,
A couple o' soul inspirin' eyes, an' the nose that
    keeps 'em apart
Is the cutest thing in the sassy line that ever
    occurred to act
As a ornament stuck on a purty face, an' that's a
    dead open fact.

I'm a-goin' to brace her by an' by to see if there's
    any hope,
To see if she's liable to shy when I'm ready to pitch
    the rope;
To see if she's goin' to make a stand, or fly like a
    skeered up dove
When I make a pass with the brandin' iron that's hot
    in the fire o' love.
I'll open the little home corral an' give her the level
    hunch
To make a run fur the open gate when I cut her out
    o' the bunch,
Fur there ain't no sense in a-jammin' 'round with a
    heart that's as soft as dough
An' a-throwin' the breath o' life away bunched up
    into sighs. Heigh-ho!

A COWBOY'S HOPELESS LOVE

James Barton Adams

I've heard that story ofttimes about that little chap
A-cryin' for the shiney moon to fall into his lap,
An' jes' a-raisin' merry hell because he couldn't git
The same to swing down low so's he could nab
    a-holt of it,
An' I'm a feelin' that-a-way, locoed I reckon, wuss
Than that same kid, though maybe not a-makin'
    sich a fuss,—
A-goin' 'round with achin' eyes a-hankerin' fer
    a peach
That's hangin' on the beauty tree, too high fer me
    to reach.

I'm jes' a rider of the range, plumb rough an'
    onrefined,
An' wild an' keerless in my ways, like others of
    my kind;
A reckless cuss in leather chaps, an' tanned an'
    blackened so
You'd think I wuz a Greaser from the plains of
    Mexico.
I never learnt to say a prayer, an' guess my
    style o' talk,
If fired off in a Sunday School would give 'em
    all a shock;
An' yet I got a-mopin' 'round as crazy as a loon
An' actin' like the story kid that bellered fer
    the moon.

I wish to God she'd never come with them bright
    laughin' eyes, —
Had never flashed that smile that seems a sunburst
    from the skies, —
Had stayed there in her city home instead o'
    comin' here
To visit at the ranch an' knock my heart plumb
    out o' gear.
I wish to God she'd talk to me in a way to fit
    the case, —
In words t'd have a tendency to hold me in
    my place, —
Instead o' bein' sociable an' actin' like she thought
Us cowboys good as city gents in clothes that's
    tailor bought.

If I would hint to her o' love, she'd hit that
    love a jar
An' laugh at sich a tough as me a-tryin' to
    rope a star;
She'd give them fluffy skirts a flirt, an' skate
    out o' my sight,
An' leave me paralyzed, — an' it'd serve me
    cussed right.
I wish she'd pack her pile o' trunks an' hit the
    city track,
An' maybe I'd recover from this violent attack;
An' in the future know enough to watch my
    feedin' ground
An' shun the loco weed o' love when there's an
    angel 'round.

THE TIED MAVERICK
Charles "Badger" Clark

Lay on the iron! the tie holds fast
And my wild record closes.
This maverick is down at last
Just roped and tied with roses.
And one small girl's to blame for it,
Yet I don't fight with shame for it —
Lay on the iron; I'm game for it,
Just roped and tied with roses.

I loped among the wildest band
Of saddle-hatin' winners —
Gay colts that never felt a brand
And scarred old outlaw sinners.
The wind was rein and guide to us;
The world was pasture wide to us
And our wild name was pride to us —
High headed bronco sinners!

So, loose and light we raced and fought
And every range we tasted
But now, since I'm corralled and caught,
I know them days were wasted.
From now, the all-day gait for me,
The trail that's hard but straight for me,
For down that trail who'll wait for me!
Ay! them old days were wasted!

But though I'm broke, I'll never be
A saddle-marked old groaner,
For never worthless bronc like me
Got such a gentle owner.
There could be colt days glad as mine
Or outlaw runs as mad as mine
Or rope-flung falls as bad as mine,
But never such an owner.

Lay on the iron, and lay it red!
I'll take it kind and clever.
Who wouldn't hold a prouder head
To wear that mark forever?
I'll never break and stray from her;
I'd starve and die away from her.
Lay on the iron — it's play from her —
And brand me hers forever!

"JEST BRING ME BACK MY COWGIRL GAL!"

S. Omar Barker

The boss he's took my gal to town
Fer a fancy hat and a low-neck gown!
Hi! Let's ketch a dogie!

She's left her hoss and her lover too —
Say, what's a puncher goin' to do?
Hi! Watch 'im roll a dogie!

It ain't because she's gone away
That makes me want to bust a stray —
Hi! Git along you dogie!

I'm jest afraid when she gits back
She'll up her nose at Cowboy Jack!
Hi! Doggone the dogies!

I ain't fergettin' how she rode,
That there's one thing my cow gal knowed.
Hi! Fer Gawd sake dogies!

The sage bresh seems to miss her too,
Its gray keeps turnin' kinder blue!
Hi! Move on ye dogies!

The boss he says he'll fire me quick
If I keeps on a-actin' sick —
Hi! Step it up ye dogies!

I answers him and says: "Old pal,
Jest bring me back my cowgirl gal!"
Hi! Let's ketch a dogie!

He says he'll bring her home frum school
Too high-toned fer a cowboy fool!
Hi! Boss watch yer dogies!

To which I says, and now repeat:
"My cowgirl gal was mighty sweet!"
Hi! I'll run his dogies!

Oh, hell, my gal's gone off to town —
If she comes back in a fancy gown —
Hi! Ye dogies, maybe!

I'll kiss her once and shoot the boss,
Then hit the trail on my old hoss!
Hi! Ye dogies, MAYBE!

FOR THE LOVE OF LILY

S. Omar Barker

Judge Bean, he cut out pictures, and he hung
    'em on the wall,
And the same fair lady's features smiled
    upon him from them all,
For beneath his barkeep's apron and behind his
    snorts at Bart,
The ol' judge felt the caperin' of a love-be-
    smitten heart.
Her name was Lily Langtry, known to fortune
    and to fame.
Bean hadn't never seen her, but he loved her just
    the same,
As above the whiskey bottles on his far-off
    frontier bar,
Her smile looked down upon him like the
    twinklin' of a star.

"By gobs," says Bean, "that lady is the world's
    most beauteous saint,
And my whippin' post's out yonder for the
    skunk that says she ain't!"
Now some there was that said it, or agreed in
    such like words
That the judge, he lawed 'em harder than if
    they'd rustled herds.
But one young puncher horsethief that ol' Bart
    fetched in for trial,
Spoke of how he'd seen her actin', and he praised
    her lovely smile,
And the judge he drunk it in and says: "By gobs,
    it's plain to me
This gent ain't stole no horses, and by gobs, I'll
    set him free!"

Thus beauty tempered justice in them days now
    long agone,
And the poor judge longed for Lily till the day
    he traveled on;
But before his grizzled whiskers shook their last
    courtroom sashay,
He renamed the village for her — and it's
    "Langtry" still today!

THE PHANTOM RANCH DREAM
Ed Steele

One night at the old Phantom rancho
On the banks of the Bright Angel stream,
I went to sleep with the bull frogs a-croakin'
And I had a most wonderful dream.

I dreamed I was the handsomest cowboy
That ever had set on a mule,
Simply a bear with the ladies
And a plumb dude wranglin' fool.

Well I dreamed I took a walk in the moonlight
I saw one of the strangest things,
Where my ol' rodee mule was a-eatin' her hay
I'll be durned if she hadn't grown wings.

She let out sort of a hee-haw
Flopped her wings to and fro
Wrung her old tail like a buzz saw
I guess she was rarin' to go.

Well I climbed on the ol' devil bareback
There was no place for my saddle to set
Then we started the durndest ride
That a cowboy had ever took yet.

When flittin' around in the Canyon
I got a most awful shock,
That ol' rodee made a four-point landin'
On top of Battle Ship rock.

There I saw a young maid in the moonlight
Filled me plumb full of sighs,
She had hair as gold as the sunset
And eyes as blue as the skies.

Then she walked right up to me
Just sort of cooed like a dove.
Said, "I've waited a long time my hero,
For a taste of this cowboy love."

Well I knew that my wreck was a-burnin'
When she laid her purty head on my chest,
And my heart made an awful commotion
In the left side of my breast.

I swore that some day I would wife her
But I never saw the end of my scheme
The alarm clock went off in the morning
And ended my dude wranglin' dream.

THE JOLLY COWBOY
(anonymous)

My lover, he is a cowboy, he's brave and kind
    and true,
He rides a Spanish pony, he throws a lasso, too;
And when he comes to see me our vows we
    do redeem,
He throws his arms around me and thus begins
    to sing:

"Ho, I'm a jolly cowboy, from Texas now I hail,
Give me my quirt and pony, I'm ready for the trail;
I love the rolling prairies, they're free from care
    and strife,
Behind a herd of longhorns I'll journey all my life.

"When early dawn is breaking and we are far away,
We fall into our saddles, we round-up all the day;
We rope, we brand, we ear-mark, I tell you we
    are smart,
And when the herd is ready, for Kansas then
    we start.

"Oh, I am a Texas cowboy, lighthearted, brave,
    and free,
To roam the wide, wide prairie, 'tis always joy to me.
My trusty little pony is my companion true,
O'er creeks and hills and rivers he's sure to pull
    me through.

"When threatening clouds do gather and herded
    lightnings flash,
And heavy rain drops splatter, and rolling
    thunders crash;
What keeps the herd from running, stampeding
    far and wide?
The cowboy's long, low whistle and singing by
    their side.

"When in Kansas City, our boss he pays us up,
We loaf around the city and take a parting cup;
We bid farewell to city life, from noisy crowds
    we come,
And back to dear old Texas, the cowboy's
    native home."

Oh, he is coming back to marry the only girl
    he loves,
He says I am his darling, I am his own true love;
Some day we two will marry and then no more
    he'll roam,
But settle down with Mary in a cozy little home.

"Ho, I'm a jolly cowboy, from Texas now I hail,
Give me my bond to Mary, I'll quit the Lone
    Star trail.
I love the rolling prairies, they're free from care
    and strife,
But I'll quit the herd of longhorns for the sake of
    my little wife."

A FRAGMENT

(anonymous)

I am fur from my sweetheart
And she is fur from me,
And when I'll see my sweetheart
I can't tell when 'twill be.

But I love her just the same,
No matter where I roam;
And that there girl will wait fur me
Whenever I come home.

I've roamed the Texas prairies,
I've followed the cattle trail,
I've rid a pitching pony
Till the hair came off his tail.

I've been to cowboy dances,
I've kissed the Texas girls,
But they ain't none what can compare
With my own sweetheart's curls.

COWBOY LOVE SONG

Gail I. Gardner

See the sun a-comin' out,
Behind the thunder showers;
Honey-chile, the mornin' loves you true.
Li'l raindrops glisten
On the painted Injun flower;
Honey-chile, the mornin' loves you true.

The muddy road is brown and still,
As far as you can see;
Honey-chile the noon-time loves you true.
A great big deer's a-watchin' us,
Beneath that cedar tree;
Honey-chile, the noontime loves you true.

The sun is sinkin' through the trees,
And leaves the clouds all red;
Honey-chile, the evenin' loves you true.
Just like I lights a nice warm fire
Before I goes to bed;
Honey-chile, the evenin' loves you true.

Old Lady Moon comes peekin' up
To see what she can see;
Honey-chile, the nighttime loves you true.
And finds you sittin' on a rock
So very close to me.
Honey-chile, I guess I loves you too.

That Letter

Bruce Kiskaddon

I rode to that box a settin' on a post beside the trail,
That our outfit used fur gettin' all their messages
    and mail.
There I got a little letter and the envelope was pink,
It shore set me feelin' better but it sorter made
    me think.
Yes, the feelin' was surprisin' onderneath my
    Stetson hat.
I could feel my hair a risin' like the bristles of a cat.

Well I tore the letter open and I read it through
    and through.
All the time I was a hopin' I would savvy what to do.
Men is quick upon the trigger, come tangle ups
    and fights,
But a woman, you caint figger what she means by
    what she writes.
It was purty and invitin' like a sunny day in spring,
She had done a heap of writin' but she hadn't said
    a thing.

Now, when men folks start to writin' you can mostly
    onderstand,
And the stuff that thay're a sightin' stands out plain
    jest like a brand
They don't never do no playin' they've a sort of
    sudden way,

For they start tight in by sayin' what they started
    out to say.
Men is given to expressin' what they mean, right then
    and there,
But a woman keeps you guessin' till your mind goes
    everywhere.

Fer a spell I'd do some thinkin' then I'd start agin
    and read;
I kept frownin' and a blinkin' till at last I got her lead.
In that letter there was lurkin' jest one simple
    plain idee.
When I got my mind a workin' it was plain enough
    to see.
Fer she said her and her mother, come a Saturday
    next week
Would be over with her brother to the dance on
    Turkey Creek.

On the start, you see, I never had no notion what
    she meant
She had fixed it up right clever in the way the
    letter went.
Man! I shore did whoop and beller when the idee hit
    me fair,
She would come without no feller and she aimed to
    meet me there.
It shore made me like her better fer that bashful gal
    of mine,
Went and built that whole durned letter jest to write
    that single line.

TONIGHT MY HEART'S IN TEXAS
(anonymous)

In the Lone Star State of Texas
By the silvery Rio Grande,
A couple strolled one evening,
Lingering hand in hand.

'Twas a ranchman's pretty daughter
And the lad she loved so dear;
On the morrow they must part
For many and many a year.

To Europe she was going
To become a lady grand,
And she went away next morning
From the silvery Rio Grande.

Her father hoped some earl
Or else a count she'd wed,
But her heart was true to Jack.
One day a letter came and thus it read:

Chorus:
Tonight my heart's in Texas
Though I'm far across the sea,
For the band is playing Dixie
And in Dixie I long to be.

Dad says some earl I'll marry,
But you have my heart and hand.
Tonight my heart's in Texas
By the silvery Rio Grande.

At a stately hall in England
Stood a Texas lass one night.
The scene was one of splendor
And the lamps were dazzling bright.

An earl knelt there before her,
Begging her to take his hand;
But her thoughts were far away
By the silvery Rio Grande.

"I can't say, 'Yes,' " she answered.
"Your title I cannot take.
There's a lad away in Texas —
They call him Texas Jack.

"Long ago I promised
That Texas lad to wed.
'Twas only yesterday I wrote,
And this the letter said:

Tonight my heart's in Texas
Though I'm far across the sea,
For the band is playing Dixie
And in Dixie I long to be.

Chapter 2

COWBOY GOES A-COURTIN'

hen the cowboy got slicked up to go courting, he might not bring a dozen roses and a sparkling diamond ring. He had his own special way with words. And even when he was struck dumb in the face of his beloved, like S. Omar Barker's Bashful Burt ("a tophand with the herd, but too ungodly modest to attempt a courtin' word") he still managed to win his heart's desire. But at no time did the cowpoke express himself as ardently as at a Saturday night dance: "If you love her tell her so / Rope her, brand her, let her go / Round her up and hold her there / Prom-'nade all, you know where."

ONE WAY OF PROPOSIN'

S. Omar Barker

Oh, Sue was young and Sue was fair and
    Sue was slim and neat.
She helped support her crippled Dad by
    servin' stuff to eat
To hungry cowboys stoppin' in, from
    wranglin' stock all weary,
And plenty of us hankered hard to have Sue
    for our dearie.

Most specially young Bashful Burt, a
    tophand with the herd,
But too ungodly modest to attempt a
    courtin' word.
She turned the rest of us plumb down, so
    sweet it hardly hurt,
And then we seen the way it was — she
    hankered after Burt!

And him all blush and bashfulness, the pore
    cowpunchin' sinner,
He had her won already but was still too
    dumb to win her.
Then one fine day a drummer guy breezed in
    for noonday chow,
And growled about the service like he
    hankered for a row.

The fare was beans — and mighty fine. I
know, for I was there.
But this here uppish drummer bowed his
neck and pawed the air.
Shoved back his beans plumb unpolite: "I
ain't no hired help!
Bring me some food that's civilized!" You
should have heard him yelp.

Pore Sue looked all beflustered. Then Burt riz
up in his jeans,
Drawed out his gun and calmly says: "Now
stranger, eat them beans!"
Then Sue looks up adorin' and toward Burt
kinder leans,
Till all at once he kisses her — and the
stranger eats his beans!

PONY TRACKS
Henry Herbert Knibbs

I was ridin' for the Blue,
When she wrote to me from France;
Wrote and sent her picture, too!
Talk about that there "Romance"!

Wrote to me, the Ridin' Kid,
Just a cattle-chasin' cuss,
But you bet I'm glad she did
Say that she had heard of us

Cowboys of the Western range;
Kinda thought that joke the best,
For we'd call it mighty strange
If the ranges weren't out West.

Sent her picture, and it's great!
Slim and neat from heel to head,
Stylish dressed and settin' straight
On a dandy thoroughbred.

Said she'd read some poetry
All about a Roan Cayuse;
Well, I own it's up to me,
I ain't makin' no excuse,

But sometimes I got to sing,
When my pony jogs along;
Seems his hoofs they click and ring
Till they've hammered out a song

Kinda like the sound of rain,
Kinda like the sun and sky,
Shadows streakin' crost the plain,
Little clouds a-floatin' by,

And a puncher and his hoss
Ridin' trails that never end . . .
Well, I showed it to the boss,
And he sent it to a friend.

Friend he owned a printin' shop,
And a high-tone magazine;
Say, my heart sure took a flop,
When that poetry I seen.

Boys they joshed me stout and strong;
Called me "Little Warblin' Kid!"
Me! I'm only six feet long
From my boot-heels to my lid.

Wonder if her eyes are brown?
Wonder if they're blue or gray?
Wonder if she lives in town?
Wonder if *she'd* ever say,

"Howdy, pardner!" Shucks! but she
Never seen a Stetson hat,
Never seen a guy like me;
And she'd never talk like that.

But I learned to say her name;
Asked the schoolmarm straight, one day;
Print and sound ain't just the same,
But it spells like this — "Edmée."

Wrote that she would like to ride
Where the world is big and free,
But she says her family's pride
Keeps her where she ought to be.

Says she's longin' for the life
Out here where the cattle roam;
Well, *I* never had a wife,
Never hung my hat to home.

Guess that letter got me hard;
Prettiest girl I ever seen;
That's what comes of singin', pard,
And a high-tone magazine.

When I'm ridin' 'round the herd,
And the stars are shinin' bright,
I keep practicin' that word,
And I aim to get it right;

"Edmée." But my pony's feet,
Keep a-arguin' and say,
Slow and steady — and repeat —
"France is — mighty — far — away!"

THE COWBOY AND THE MAID

(anonymous)

Funny how it come about!
Me and Texas Tom was out
Takin' of a moonlight walk,
Fillin' in the time with talk.
Every star up in the sky
Seemed to wink the other eye
At each other, 'sif they
Smelt a mouse around our way!

Me and Tom had never grew
Spoony like some couples do;
Never billed and cooed and sighed;
He was bashful like and I'd
Notions of my own that it
Wasn't policy to git
Too abundant till I'd got
Of my feller good and caught.

As we walked along that night
He got talkin' of the bright
Prospects that he had, and I
Somehow felt, I dunno why,
That a-fore we cake-walked back
To the ranch he'd make a crack
Fer my hand, and I was plum
Achin' fer the shock to come.

By and by he says, "I've got
Fifty head o' cows, and not
One of 'em but, on the dead,
Is a crackin' thoroughbred.

Got a daisy claim staked out,
And I'm thinkin' it's about
Time fer me to make a shy
At a home." "O Tom!" says I.

"Bin a-lookin' 'round," says he,
"Quite a little while to see
'F I could git a purty face
Fer to ornament the place.
Plenty of 'em in the land;
But the one 'at wears my brand
Must be sproutin' wings to fly!"
"You deserve her, Tom," says I.

"Only one so fur," says he,
"Fills the bill, and mebbe she
Might shy off and bust my hope
If I should pitch the poppin' rope.
Mebbe she'd git hot an' say
That it was a silly play
Askin' her to make a tie."
"She would be a fool," says I.

'Tain't nobody's business what
Happened then, but I jist thought
I could see the moon-man smile
Cutely down upon us, while
Me and him was walkin' back, —
Stoppin' now and then to smack
Lips rejoicin' that at last
The dread crisis had been past.

THE COWBOY'S VALENTINE

C.F. Lummis

Say, Moll, now don't you 'llow to quit
A-playin' maverick?
Sech stock should be corralled a bit
An' hev a mark 't 'll stick.

Old Val's a-roundin'-up today
Upon the Sweetheart Range,
'N me a-helpin', so to say,
Though this yere herd is strange

To me 'n yit, ef I c'd rope
Jes *one* to wear my brand
I'd strik f'r Home Ranch on a lope,
The happiest in the land.

Yo' savvy who I'm runnin' so,
Yo' savvy who I be;
Now, can't yo' take that brand — yo' know, —
The ♥ M-I-N-E.

TO DANCE WITH HER

Robert V. Carr

To dance with her rounds-up such bliss,
I can't rope words to half explain;
It's so blamed sweet it seems to be
A second cousin to a pain.
She drifts an' leans agin my arm —
Sweetheart an' dreams an' music fine —
If anything is better, say!
I'd choke with joy if it was mine.

TIME'S HEAVY HAND

Robert V. Carr

She was jes' a little granger an' her folks
    lived on Elk crick,
Jes' a little dark-eyed granger, but she
    allers drest that slick
You'd think she'd caught the fashion from
    the ladies o' the town,
'Specially when buggy-ridin' in her
    Sunday-meetin' gown.

Uster take her 'way out drivin' on a
    Sunday, don't you know,
But I'd let her do the drivin', fer I liked
    it better so;
An' then my arm would circle — huh,
    she'd pertend to frown —
The place what was the smallest in her
    Sunday-meetin' gown.

Starlight, yes, an' prairies dreamin',
    cottonwoods a-sighin' there,
An' the wind a sort o' triflin' an' a-foolin'
    with her hair;
An' a ribbin on my shoulder or a strayin'
    curl o' brown,
An' her heart a-beatin' gently 'gin her
    Sunday-meetin' gown.

Uster kiss her — huh, well, sort o' —
    when the moon got back a cloud,
An' she'd pout her lips pertendin' she was
    mad an' then aloud
She'd laff an' fix her ribbins, fer at times
    such things come down
When a girl goes buggy-ridin' in her
    Sunday meetin' gown.

Goodness my! but time's skeedaddled; jes'
    a-driftin' that-o-way,
I'm bald-headed — gettin' worser ev'ry
    single passin' day;
An' mother, oh, well, mother busts the
    scales up in the town,
An' she's made herself a necktie of that
    Sunday-meetin' gown.

An' A Two-Step's What They Play

Robert V. Carr

A little queen in calico,
Her smiles — them killin' smiles —
Be jes' some o' a thousand
Of her wicked ways an' wiles;
An' she's the smoothest dancer
'Most anywhere you'll see,
An' you ought to see her two-step,
La-de-da, along with me.

Oh, she's light as any feather,
The music's simply fine,
An' I jes' get plum' loco
When her face is close to mine.
Fer my heart is thinkin' something
My lips don't dast to say,
When she leans agin my shoulder
An' a two-step's what they play.

I could dance with her ferever,
Wisht we never'd get thro',
'Cause Time jes' takes a lay-off,
An' reason quits work, too.
Seems ev'rything has ended,
Fer a spell fergot to be,
When they plays a two-step sweetly
An' she drifts away with me.

DOWN AT HALLER'S DANCIN'

Robert V. Carr

They're tunin' up the orchestray down at
    old Bill Haller's;
He's the feller that they claim jes' beats all
    the callers
In the country 'round fer miles — old
    bow-legged feller;
Say, you ought to hear that cuss jes' get up
    an' beller:

Balance all an' do-see-do,
Rope her, tie her, let her go,
Mill her 'round an' kiss her there,
Prom'nade all, you know where.

Choose your partners! H-m-m-m! well, yes,
    grab the next one after,
'Twon't harm nothin' if you do shake the roof
    with lafter;
Fer she's joy-time, whoop-hi-ree! Come
    around a-prancin',
Guess there's nothin' like the time down at
    Haller's dancin'.

She's your true love, you can bet,
There's no dead ones in that set!
Lope her 'round an' squeeze her there,
Prom'nade all, you know where.

Hear them fiddles! Hain't they great! Suff'rin'
    Land o' Lawdy!
Ragtime, night time, high time, too, come a-
    steppin' gawdy.
Come a-sailin' down the line, whoop-a-lorum!
    let her,
Seems to me there's nothin' that makes a man
    feel better.

Mornin' is a mile away,
Never 'spect to hit the hay,
She's a-waitin', wake up there!
Prom'nade all, you know where.

Hear old Haller, hear him now, all above
    the funnin',
Jes' a-laffin', callin', too, keeps the thing
    a-runnin',
Round me up and turn me loose! Let me
    go a-prancin';
All I want is jes' to yell down at Haller's
    dancin'.

If you love her tell her so,
Rope her, brand her, let her go;
Round her up an' hold her there,
Prom'nade all, you know where.

AT A COWBOY DANCE

James Barton Adams

Git yo' little sagehens ready;
Trot 'em out upon the floor —
Line up there, you critters! Steady!
Lively, now! One couple more.
Shorty, shed that ol' sombrero;
Broncho, douse that cigaret;
Stop yer cussin', Casimero,
'Fore the ladies. Now, all set:

S'lute yer ladies, all together;
Ladies opposite the same;
Hit the lumber with yer leather;
Balance all an' swing yer dame;
Bunch the heifers in the middle;
Circle stags an' do-ce-do;
Keep a-steppin' to the fiddle;
Swing 'em 'round an' off you go.

First four forward. Back to places.
Second foller. Shuffle back —
Now you've got it down to cases —
Swing 'em till their trotters crack.
Gents all right a-heel an' toein';
Swing 'em — kiss 'em if yo' kin —
On to next an' keep a-goin'
Till yo' hit yer pards agin.

Gents to center. Ladies 'round 'em;
Form a basket; balance all;
Swing yer sweets to where yo' found 'em;
All p'mnade around the hall.
Balance to yer pards and trot 'em
'Round the circle double quick;
Grab an' squeeze 'em while you've got 'em —
Hold 'em to it if they kick.

Ladies, left hand to yer sonnies;
Alaman; grand right an' left;
Balance all an' swing yer honies —
Pick 'em up an' feel their heft.
All p'mnade like skeery cattle;
Balance all an' swing yer sweets;
Shake yer spurs an' make 'em rattle —
Keno! Promenade to seats.

THE GIRL THAT WORE A WATERFALL

(anonymous)

Come all young men who've been in love and
    sympathize with me,
For I have loved as fair a maid as ever you
    did see.
Her age it was but seventeen, a figure fair
    and tall,
She was a handsome creature and she wore
    a waterfall.

The first time that I met her, I never shall
    forget,
I'd slipped into a dry goods store some
    handkerchiefs to get.
She stood behind the counter dressed up just
    like a doll,
I never saw a face so fair or such a waterfall.

'Twas at a picnic party, I met her after that,
I quickly introduced myself; we had a
    pleasant chat.
Though many other girls were there, yet
    none of them at all
Could dance with me except the girl who
    wore the waterfall.

[61]

I saw her home, we marched along, we said
    we'd never part,
And when she asked me to come in, I found
    I'd lost my heart;
While sitting there I thought I heard some
    footsteps in the hall,
All sorts of colors turned the girl who wore
    the waterfall.

A great big fellow six feet high came
    stalking in the room,
And when he saw me sitting there at once
    began to fume.
His eyes so hard, his face so harsh, it did
    my heart appall —
"This is my husband," said the girl who wore
    the waterfall.

Before I'd time to say a word, the fellow
    at me flew,
And while the maid held me down, he beat
    me black and blue.
When I got up I found I'd lost watch, money,
    chain and all —
I never since go near a girl who wears
    a waterfall.

Chapter 3

THE HEARTBROKE COWBOY

Abandoned, jilted by the loves they lost, cowboy and cowgirl poets were especially expressive when their hearts were broken. Cowboying didn't allow for a stable love life — the girls they left behind often married another. The resulting poetry was sometimes as mournful as the pitiful bawl of a lost calf. Other times the poems were filled with righteous indignation, as the broken-hearted poets preached about the perils of a false-hearted lover.

RED RIVER VALLEY
(anonymous)

From this valley they say you are goin',
I will miss your bright eyes and sweet smile.
For they say you are takin' the sunshine
That has brightened my path for awhile.

Chorus:
Come and sit by my side if you love me.
Do not hasten to bid me adieu.
Just remember the Red River Valley
And this cowboy that loves you so true.

From this valley they say you are goin',
I will miss your sweet face and sweet smile.
Just because you are weary and tired,
You're a-changin' your range for awhile.

Chorus

I've been waitin' a long time my darlin'
For the sweet words you never did say.
Now at last my fond hopes have vanished,
For they say that you're goin' away.

Chorus

O there never could be such a longin'
In the heart of a poor cowboy's breast.
That now dwells in this heart you're a-breakin'
As I wait in my home in the West.

Chorus

Do you think of the valley you're leavin'
And how lonely and gray it will be?
Do you think of the kind heart you're breakin',
And the sad pain you're causin' for me?

Chorus

As you go to your home by the ocean,
May you never forget those sweet hours
That we spent in this Red River Valley,
And the love we exchanged mid the flowers.

Chorus

LONESOME

S. Omar Barker

Oh, there's someone I'll be missin'
When the moon comes, mesa-kissin',
Out o' twilight hills that tender way it knows.
An' the coyotes starts to holler
Down the trail we used to foller,
Ridin' side by side, our boots jes' touchin' toes.

Through the day I'm busy ropin',
But at dusk my heart goes lopin'
To the sagebrush mesa where we used to meet.
Ridin' range weren't never lonely
Till she came — an' left. It's only
Missin' her that makes the moonlight
    incomplete.

BUCKING BRONCHO
Belle Starr

My love is a rider, wild bronchos he breaks,
Though he's promised to quit it, just for my sake.
He ties up one foot, the saddle puts on,
With a swing and a jump he is mounted and gone.

The first time I met him, 'twas early one spring,
Riding a broncho, a high-headed thing.
He tipped me a wink as he gaily did go;
For he wished me to look at his bucking broncho.

The next time I saw him 'twas late in the fall,
Swinging the girls at Tomlinson's ball.
He laughed and he talked as we danced to and fro,
Promised never to ride on another broncho.

He made me some presents, among them a ring;
The return that I made him was a far better thing;
'Twas a young maiden's heart, I'd have you all know;
He's won it by riding his bucking broncho.

My love has a gun, and the gun he can use,
But he's quit his gun fighting as well as his booze;
And he's sold him his saddle, his spurs, and his rope,
And there's no more cow punching, and that's what I hope.

My love has a gun that has gone to the bad,
Which makes poor old Jimmy feel pretty damn sad;
For the gun it shoots high and the gun it shoots low,
And it wobbles about like a bucking broncho.

Now all you young maidens, where'er you reside,
Beware of the cowboy who swings the raw-hide;
He'll court you and pet you and leave you and go
In the spring up the trail on his bucking broncho.

A Bad Half Hour

Charles "Badger" Clark

Wonder why I feel so restless;
Moon is shinin' still and bright,
Cattle all is restin' easy,
But I just kain't sleep tonight.
Ain't no cactus in my blankets,
Don't know why they feel so hard —
'Less it's Warblin' Jim a-singin'
"Annie Laurie" out on guard.

"Annie Laurie" — wish he'd quit it!
Couldn't sleep now if I tried.
Makes the night seem big and lonesome,
And my throat feels sore inside.
How my Annie used to sing it!
And it sounded good and gay
Nights I drove her home from dances
When the east was turnin' gray.

Yes, "her brow was like the snowdrift"
And her eyes like quiet streams,
"And her face" — I still kin see it
Much too frequent in my dreams;

And her hand was soft and trembly
That night underneath the tree,
When I couldn't help but tell her
She was "all the world to me."

But her folks said I was "shif'less,"
"Wild," "unsettled," — they was right,
For I leaned to punchin' cattle
And I'm at it still tonight.
And she married young Doc Wilkins —
Oh my Lord! but that was hard!
Wish that fool would quit his singin'
"Annie Laurie" out on guard!

Oh, I just kain't stand it thinkin'
Of the things that happened then.
Good old times, and all apast me!
Never seem to come again —
My turn? Sure. I'll come a runnin'.
Warm me up some coffee, pard —
But I'll stop that Jim from singin'
"Annie Laurie" out on guard.

A BORDER AFFAIR

Charles "Badger" Clark

Spanish is the lovin' tongue,
Soft as music, light as spray;
'Twas a girl I learnt it from
Livin' down Sonora way.
I don't look much like a lover,
Yet I say her love-words over
Often, when I'm all alone —
"Mi amor, mi corazón."

Nights when she knew where I'd ride
She would listen for my spurs,
Throw the big door open wide,
Raise them laughin' eyes of hers,
And my heart would nigh stop beatin'
When I'd hear her tender greetin'
Whispered soft for me alone —
"Mi amor! mi corazón!"

Moonlight in the patio,
Old Señora noddin' near,
Me and Juana talkin' low
So the "madre" couldn't hear —
How those hours would go aflyin',
And too soon I'd hear her sighin',
In her little sorry-tone —
"Adios, mi corazón."

But one time I had to fly
For a foolish gamblin' fight,
And we said a swift good-bye
On that black, unlucky night.
When I'd loosed her arms from clingin',
With her words the hoofs kept ringin',
As I galloped north alone —
"Adios, mi corazón."

Never seen her since that night;
I kaint cross the Line, you know.
She was Mex. and I was white;
Like as not it's better so.
Yet I've always sort of missed her
Since that last, wild night I kissed her,
Left her heart and lost my own —
"Adios, mi corazón."

A Cowpunch Courtship

E.A. Brininstool

She got me clean stampeded
An' locoed to a turn;
I ought to have heeded
Them fetchin' ways o' her'n.
I might have knowed for certain
She'd git the bulge on me,
When I commenced a-flirtin'
With her so all-fired free.

She was a peach, a pippin,
An' 'twasn't nothin' strange
That I commenced a-skippin'
Across onto her range;
I shouldn't gone cavortin'
On her bed-ground, I know,
Head up an' jest a-snortin'
To hog-tie her, you know.

You see at this here love-game
I wasn't halter-broke;
'Twas new to me — this dove game,
I liked it — that's no joke!
An' when I started chasin'
Around in her corral,
'Twasn't long 'fore I was facin'
Conditions that was hell!

I told her I was ready
To slap on her my brand,
She was close-herded steady
By this love-sick cow-hand.
But jes' when I was tryin'
To slip on her my noose,
Why, she commenced a-shyin'
An' framin' an excuse.

. . . .

The boys ain't quit their naggin';
They're rubbin' on me raw;
My under lip is saggin'
The wirst you ever saw.
There's reason for it, maybe,
But 'twon't occur again —
She's married, an' her baby
An' ol' man's in Cheyenne!

THE MAN YOU COULDN'T GET

Robert V. Carr

You can cry and you can try,
To the very day you die,
Turnin' up a haughty nose —
Sort o' scornful, I suppose,
But you're still a-dreamin' yet
Of the man you couldn't get.

Most as likely some day you
Will get married — hope you do —
An' your proud neck bend to rub
Little dresses in a tub;
But somehow I place this bet:
Him you never will ferget.

Course you knows time's comin' that
You'll be homely, old an' fat;
Then your man will wonder why
Once a great while that you sigh;
Well you knows what makes you fret,
Even then you can't ferget.

Husband, yes, he'll wonder why
That you turn a-drift a sigh,
Tho' he'll feel it sort o' dim,
That the said sigh hain't fer him —
It's fer one you love some yet:
Fer the man you couldn't get.

He don't care, fer 'tis true,
He jes' sort o' thinks o' you,
As a girl he uster know —
One o' many, sure, that's so.
But you're longin', sighin' yet,
Fer the man you couldn't get.

Can't ferget that night that you
Loved him long an' sweet an' true,
Can't ferget his voice an' style,
Reckless, careless all the while,
Can't ferget that old dark day,
When he laffed and walked away.

RAMBLING BOY

(anonymous)

I am a wild and roving lad,
A wild and rambling lad I'll be;
For I do love a little girl
And she does love me.

"O Willie, O Willie, I love you so,
I love you more than I do know;
And if my tongue could tell you so
I'd give the world to let you know."

When Julia's old father came this to know, –
That Julia and Willie were loving so, –
He ripped and swore among them all,
And swore he'd use a cannon ball.

She wrote Willie a letter with her right hand
And sent it to him in the western land.
"Oh, read these lines, sweet William dear.
For this is the last of me you will hear."

He read those lines while he wept and cried,
"Ten thousand times I wish I had died."
He read those lines while he wept and said,
"Ten thousand times I wish I were dead."

When her old father came home that night
He called for Julia, his heart's delight,
He ran up stairs and her door he broke
And found her hanging by her own bed rope.

And with his knife he cut her down,
And in her bosom this note he found
Saying, "Dig my grave both deep and wide
And bury sweet Willie by my side."

They dug her grave both deep and wide
And buried sweet Willie by her side;
And on her grave set a turtle dove
To show the world they died for love.

THE RAMBLING COWBOY

K. Tolliver

There was a rich old rancher who lived in the
country by,
He had a lovely daughter on whom I cast
my eye;
She was pretty, tall, and handsome, both neat
and very fair,
There's no other girl in the country with her
I could compare.

I asked her if she would be willing for me to
cross the plains;
She said she would be truthful until I returned
again;
She said she would be faithful until death did
prove unkind,
So we kissed, shook hands, and parted, and I
left my girl behind.

I left the State of Texas, for Arizona I was
bound;
I landed in Tombstone City, I viewed the place
all 'round.
Money and work were plentiful and the
cowboys they were kind
But the only thought of my heart was the girl
I left behind.

One day as I was riding across the public
     square
The mailcoach came in and I met the driver
     there;
He handed me a letter which gave me to
     understand
That the girl I left in Texas had married
     another man.

I turned myself all 'round and about not
     knowing what to do,
But I read on down some further and it proved
     the words were true.
Hard work I have laid over, it's gambling
     I have designed.
I'll ramble this wide world over for the girl
     I left behind.

Come all you reckless and rambling boys who
     have listened to this song,
If it hasn't done you any good, it hasn't done
     you any wrong;
But when you court a pretty girl, just marry
     her while you can,
For if you go across the plains she'll marry
     another man.

THE TRAIL TO MEXICO
(anonymous)

I made up my mind to change my way
And quit my crowd that was so gay,
To leave my native home for a while
And to travel west for many a mile.

Whoo-a-whoo-a-whoo-a-whoo.

'Twas all in the merry month of May
When I started for Texas far away,
I left my darling girl behind,
She said her heart was only mine.

Whoo-a-whoo-a-whoo-a-whoo.

Oh, it was when I embraced her in my arms
I thought she had ten thousand charms;
Her caresses were soft, her kisses were sweet,
Saying, "We will get married next time we meet."

Whoo-a-whoo-a-whoo-a-whoo.

It was in the year of eighty-three
That A. J. Stinson hired me.
He said, "Young fellow, I want you to go
And drive this herd to Mexico."

Whoo-a-whoo-a-whoo-a-whoo.

The first horse they gave me was an old black
With two big set-fasts on his back;
I padded him with gunny-sacks and my bedding all;
He went up, then down, and I got a fall.

Whoo-a-whoo-a-whoo-a-whoo.

The next they gave me was an old gray,
I'll remember him till my dying day.
And if I had to swear to the fact,
I believe he was worse off than the black.

Whoo-a-whoo-a-whoo-a-whoo.

Oh, it was early in the year
When I went on trail to drive the steer.
I stood my guard through sleet and snow
While on the trail to Mexico.

Whoo-a-whoo-a-whoo-a-whoo.

Oh, it was a long and lonesome go
As our herd rolled on to Mexico;
With laughter light and the cowboy's song
To Mexico we rolled along.

Whoo-a-whoo-a-whoo-a-whoo.

When I arrived in Mexico
I wanted to see my love but could not go;
So I wrote a letter, a letter to my dear,
But not a word from her could I hear.

Whoo-a-whoo-a-whoo-a-whoo.

When I arrived at the once loved home
I called for the darling of my own;
They said she had married a richer life,
Therefore, wild cowboy, seek another wife.

Whoo-a-whoo-a-whoo-a-whoo.

Oh, the girl she is married I do adore,
And I cannot stay at home any more;
I'll cut my way to a foreign land
Or I'll go back west to my cowboy band.

Whoo-a-whoo-a-whoo-a-whoo.

I'll go back to the Western land,
I'll hunt up my old cowboy band, —
Where the girls are few and the boys are true
And a false-hearted love I never knew.

Whoo-a-whoo-a-whoo-a-whoo.

"O Buddie, O Buddie, please stay at home,
Don't be forever on the roam.
There is many a girl more true than I,
So pray don't go where the bullets fly."

Whoo-a-whoo-a-whoo-a-whoo.

"It's curse your gold and your silver too,
God pity a girl that won't prove true;
I'll travel West where the bullets fly,
I'll stay on the trail till the day I die."

Whoo-a-whoo-a-whoo-a-whoo.

LACKEY BILL
(anonymous)

Come all you good old boys and listen to my rhymes,
We are west of Eastern Texas and mostly men of crimes;
Each with a hidden secret well smothered in his breast,
Which brought us out to Mexico, way out here in
     the West.

My parents raised me tenderly, they had no child but me,
Till I began to ramble and with them could never agree.
My mind being bent on rambling did grieve their poor
     hearts sore,
To leave my aged parents them to see no more.

I was borned and raised in Texas, though never come
     to fame,
A cowboy by profession, C.W. King, by name.
Oh, when the war was ended I did not like to work,
My brothers were not happy, for I had learned to shirk.

In fact I was not able, my health was very bad,
I had no constitution, I was nothing but a lad.
I had no education, I would not go to school,
And living off my parents I thought it rather cool.

So I set a resolution to travel to the West,
My parents they objected, but still I thought it best.
It was out on the Seven Rivers all out on the Pecos stream,
It was there I saw a country I thought just suited me.

I thought I would be no stranger and lead a civil life,
In order to be happy would choose myself a wife.
On one Sabbath evening in the merry month of May,
To a little country singing I happened there to stray.

It was there I met a damsel I never shall forget,
The impulse of that moment remains within me yet.
We soon became acquainted, I thought she would
    fill the bill,
She seemed to be good-natured, which helps to climb
    the hill.

She was a handsome figure though not so very tall;
Her hair was red as blazes, I hate it worst of all.
I saw her home one evening in the presence of her pap,
I bid them both good evening with a note left in her lap.

And when I got an answer I read it with a rush,
I found she had consented, my feelings was a hush.
But now I have changed my mind, boys, I am sure
    I wish her well.
Here's to that precious jewel, I'm sure I wish her well.

This girl was Miss Mollie Walker who fell in love with me,
She was a lovely Western girl, as lovely as could be,
She was so tall, so handsome, so charming and so fair,
There is not a girl in this whole world with her
    I could compare.

She said my pockets would be lined with gold, hard work
    then I'd leave o'er

If I'd consent to live with her and say I'd roam no more.
My mind began to ramble and it grieved my poor heart sore.
To leave my darling girl, her to see no more.

I asked if it made any difference if I crossed o'er
    the plains;
She said it made no difference if I returned again.
So we kissed, shook hands, and parted, I left that girl
    behind.
She said she'd prove true to me till death proved her
    unkind.

I rode in the town of Vagus, all in the public square;
The mail coach had arrived, the post boy met me there.
He handed me a letter that gave me to understand
That the girl I loved in Texas had married another man.

So I read a little farther and found those words were true.
I turned myself all around, not knowing what to do.
I'll sell my horse, saddle, and bridle, cowdriving I'll resign,
I'll search this world from town to town for the girl I
    left behind.

Here the gold I find in plenty, the girls to me are kind,
But my pillow is haunted with the girl I left behind.
It's trouble and disappointment is all that I can see,
For the dearest girl in all the world has gone square
    back on me.

Joe Bowers
(anonymous)

My name is Joe Bowers,
I've got a brother Ike,
I came here from Missouri,
Yes, all the way from Pike.
I'll tell you why I left there
And how I came to roam,
And leave my poor old mammy,
So far away from home.

I used to love a gal there,
Her name was Sallie Black,
I asked her for to marry me,
She said it was a whack.
She says to me, "Joe Bowers,
Before you hitch for life,
You ought to have a little home
To keep your little wife."

Says I, "My dearest Sallie,
O Sallie, for your sake,
I'll go to California
And try to raise a stake."
Says she to me, "Joe Bowers,
You are the chap to win,
Give me a kiss to seal the bargain," —
And I throwed a dozen in.

I'll never forget my feelings
When I bid adieu to all.
Sal, she cotched me 'round the neck

And I began to bawl.
When I begun they all commenced,
You never heard the like,
How they all took on and cried
The day I left old Pike.

When I got to this here country
I hadn't nary a red,
I had such wolfish feelings
I wished myself most dead.
At last I went to mining,
Put in my biggest licks,
Came down upon the boulders
Just like a thousand bricks.

I worked both late and early
In rain and sun and snow,
But I was working for my Sallie
So 'twas all the same to Joe.
I made a very lucky strike
As the gold itself did tell,
For I was working for my Sallie,
The girl I loved so well.

But one day I got a letter
From my dear, kind brother Ike;
It came from old Missouri,
Yes, all the way from Pike.
It told me the goldarndest news
That ever you did hear,
My heart it is a-bustin'
So please excuse this tear.

I'll tell you what it was, boys,
You'll bust your sides I know;
For when I read that letter
You ought to seen poor Joe.
My knees gave 'way beneath me,
And I pulled out half my hair;
And if you ever tell this now,
You bet you'll hear me swear.

It said my Sallie was fickle,
Her love for me had fled,
That she had married a butcher,
Whose hair was awful red;
It told me more than that,
It's enough to make me swear, –
It said that Sallie had a baby
And the baby had red hair.

Now I've told you all that I can tell
About this sad affair,
'Bout Sallie marrying the butcher
And the baby had red hair.
But whether it was a boy or girl
The letter never said,
It only said its cussed hair
Was inclined to be red.

Chapter 4

LEGENDS OF LOVE ON THE RANGE

We cannot say if Indian Queen Chipeta really took a heroic ride on her chestnut steed or if Lasca indeed threw herself over her cowboy lover to shelter him from a thundering herd of cattle. But these and other dramatic tales of heroism, love and sacrifice were the inspiration for countless romantic poems and songs. Most of these were swapped around a blazing campfire under a star-filled western sky long ago, but today when they are recited before audiences of thousands at modern-day poetry gatherings, it's obvious that time has not eroded their appeal.

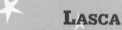

LASCA

Frank Desprez

I want free life, and I want fresh air;
And I sigh for the canter after the cattle,
The crack of the whips like shots in battle,
The medley of hoofs and horns and heads
That wars and wrangles and scatters and spreads;
The green beneath and the blue above,
And dash and danger, and life and love —
And Lasca!

Lasca used to ride
On a mouse-grey mustang close to my side,
With blue serape and bright-belled spur;
I laughed with joy as I looked at her!
Little knew she of books or creeds;
An Ave Maria sufficed her needs;
Little she cared save to be at my side,
To ride with me, and ever to ride,
From San Saba's shore to Lavaca's tide.
She was as bold as the billows that beat,
She was as wild as the breezes that blow:
From her little head to her little feet,
She was swayed in her suppleness to and fro
By each gust of passion; a sapling pine
That grows on the edge of a Kansas bluff
And wars with the wind when the weather is rough,
Is like this Lasca, this love of mine.

She would hunger that I might eat,
Would take the bitter and leave me the sweet;
But once, when I made her jealous for fun
At something I whispered or looked or done,
One Sunday, in San Antonio,
To a glorious girl in the Alamo,
She drew from her garter a little dagger,
And — sting of a wasp — it made me stagger!
An inch to the left, or an inch to the right,
And I shouldn't be maundering here tonight;
But she sobbed, and sobbing, so quickly bound
Her torn rebosa about the wound
That I swiftly forgave her. Scratches don't count
In Texas, down by the Rio Grande.

Her eye was brown — a deep, deep brown;
Her hair was darker than her eye;
And something in her smile and frown,
Curled crimson lip and instep high,
Showed that there ran in each blue vein,
Mixed with the milder Aztec strain,
The vigorous vintage of Old Spain.
She was alive in every limb
With feeling, to the finger tips;
And when the sun is like a fire,
And sky one shining, soft sapphire
One does not drink in little sips.

. . . .

The air was heavy, the night was hot,
I sat by her side and forgot, forgot;
Forgot the herd that were taking their rest,
Forgot that the air was close oppressed,
That the Texas norther comes sudden and soon,
In the dead of the night or the blaze of the noon;
That, once let the herd at its breath take fright,
Nothing on earth can stop their flight;
And woe to the rider, and woe to the steed,
That falls in front of their mad stampede!

. . . .

Was that thunder? I grasped the cord
Of my swift mustang without a word.
I sprang to the saddle, and she clung behind.
Away! on a hot chase down the wind!
But never was foxhunt half so hard,
And never was steed so little spared.
For we rode for our lives. You shall hear how we fared
In Texas, down by the Rio Grande.

The mustang flew, and we urged him on;
There was one chance left, and you have but one —
Halt, jump to the ground, and shoot your hose;
Crouch under his carcass, and take your chance;
And if the steers in their frantic course
Don't batter you both to pieces at once,
You may thank your star; if not, goodbye
To the quickening kiss and the long-drawn sigh,
And the open air and the open sky,
In Texas, down by the Rio Grande.

The cattle gained on us, and, just as I felt
For my old sixshooter behind in my belt,
Down came the mustang, and down came we,
Clinging together — and, what was the rest?
A body that spread itself on my breast,
Two arms that shielded my dizzy head,
Two lips that hard to my lips were prest;
Then came thunder in my ears,
As over us surged the sea of steers,
Blows that beat blood into my eyes,
And when I could rise —
Lasca was dead!

. . . .

I gouged out a grave a few feet deep,
And there in the Earth's arms I laid her to sleep;
And there she is lying, and no one knows;
And the summer shines, and the winter snows;
For many a day the flowers have spread
A pall of petals over her head;
And the little grey hawk hangs aloft in the air,
And the sly coyote trots here and there,
And the black snake glides and glitters and slides
Into the rift of a cotttonwood tree;
And the buzzard sails on,
And comes and is gone,
Stately and still, like a ship at sea.
And I wonder why I do not care
For the things that are, like the things that were.
Does half my heart lie buried there
In Texas, down by the Rio Grande.

OLD SAN ANTONE

Henry Herbert Knibbs

In Texas town of San Antone the Rose of Alvarado grew
From bud to early Southern bloom; her sire's delight, a
    lissome flame:
Each splendid suitor for his own her beauty and her
    laughter knew,
But none her heart till from the North a blue-eyed
    Caballero came.

His broad sombrero, twinkling spur, his rein-chains
    ringing silver-sweet,
She knew along the morning way. And he, light-
    hearted, lithe and tall,
Beheld the Rose and smiled at her. Day long she viewed
    an empty street,
Yet evening found his pony tied near Alvarado's
    garden wall.

Old San Antone beneath the moon slow creeping past
    the portal white:
"Ah, mi amor! Mi corazón!" So Alvarado's daughter sang
An Andalusian lover's tune. So clear the stars,
    so still the night!
When, tinkling to an alien stride a rowel on the
    pathway rang.

"Ah, mi amor! Mi corazón!" Twain shadows through
    the garden passed,
The belted rider of the North, a stranger in
    forbidden land,
And she, the Rose of San Antone. A whisper, "You have
    come at last!"

And from the dark mantilla's fold the flutter of
    a little hand.

None but the stars were there to hear. Her *Caballero*
    bowed his head,
As she, on tiptoe, trembling up, in instant fire of
    rapture yearned;
He laughed away her uttered fear and gave a promise
    in its stead,
While softly over San Antone the moon of summer
    midnight burned.

Faint grew the stars, and they were gone. The hidden
    roses slowly drew
From shadowy trellis to the light, as though they
    sought a vanished face,
Peering across the desert dawn and listening for a
    voice they knew,
While gray, old Alvarado mourned within his silent
    garden place.

. . . .

Vanished the Rose long years ago; vanished the garden
    of delight;
Forgotten is the lover's tune; and from the soundless
desert floor,
Sand drifts across the patio. . . . So clear the stars, so
    still the night!
Old San Antone beneath the moon: "*Mi corazón!*
    Ah, mi amor!"

LILY OF THE WEST
(anonymous)

As I went down to Louisville some pleasure for to find,
There came a girl from Lexingtown so pleasing to
    my mind;
Her hair was laid in diamonds and a star upon
    her breast,
They called her handsome Mary, the Lily of the West.

She had rings on every finger that come from the
    distant shores,
Ten thousand hundred dollars laid up for her in store;
'Tis enough to entice the king of Press, how costly
    she did dress,
And I called her my sweet Mary, the Lily of the West.

I courted her for a long time, her love I expected to gain,
Until she turned her back to me and I to her the same;
But I never shall forget that day the clod lie on my breast
And I talked to my sweet Mary, the Lily of the West.

One day when I was a-walking down by the shady grove,
There come a man from Lexingtown, come dashing
    with my love;
He sung a song most melodious, it did my soul depress,
And he called her his sweet Mary, the Lily of the West.

My rifle on my shoulder, my dagger in my hand,
I caught him by the collar while bold I bid him stand;
Me being mad and desperated, I quickly pierced
    his breast,
For talking to my Mary, the Lily of the West.

They took me to the Justice, he only but made my plea,
The jury found me innocent, the judges set me free.
And they did not say more or less
Begone you scornfulish Mary; the Lily of the West.

There was a man among them that was so honorable
      mean,
He had me bound down in iron chains and brought
      me back again;
They put me in the guard house, my life to explore,
There are spies at every window, boys, and six at
      every door.

I went around in the guard house, I surveyed it
      around and around,
I jumped out at one window and knocked five of
      them down;
The footmen and the horsemen they quickly
      followed me,
But I wheeled old Jack four times around and gained
      my liberty.

I've traveled through the westerns, I've traveled
      America through,
And a-many pretty cottage girl has come into my view;
But I never shall forget that day the clod lie on
      my breast
And I talked to my sweet Mary, the Lily of the West.

CHIPETA'S RIDE

John W. Taylor

From mountains covered deep with snow,
Uncompahgre's clear, bright waters flow,
Down which they plunge, leap and surge and roar,
Then on they sweep by a cabin door,
Where once dwelt Ouray, the king of the land
With Chipeta, his queen, brave and grand.
This brave, wise chief, and his Wild West queen,
Here lived and loved in that home serene.

The setting sun in the golden west,
Had said "Good night" to this home so blessed,
A silence hangs o'er that darkened vale,
Is broken by hoofbeats on the trail,
A weary horse flecked with dust and foam,
Staggers, falls dead, at this chieftain's home,
A courier from the dead steed sprang —
His words in the ear of the chief rang:

"Thornburg and most of his men are slain!
Meeker and his men lie dead on the plain!
The survivors led by Captain Payne,
Whose name should adorn the scroll of fame —
Behind great piles of dead horses lie,
If help comes not soon those boys will die!
Shots fired from the guns of Colorow's braves
Are fast sending them to Wild West graves.

"The four fair women of Meeker's land,
Are captives of Douglas and his band,
Who in passion vile, with cruel hands
Will wrest from them virtue God demands.
A thousand miners in yon high hills,
Their cries for vengeance all this land now fills,
If men who behind those horses lie,
By bullets shot by red hands should die.

"Or should those white women be defiled
To satisfy lust of brutes so wild,
Not a Ute will live to tell the tale,
Or chase the deer o'er mountain trail."

At the words the Chief from his couch then sprang,
His words through the silent night then rang —
"Bring my horse, I ride to stop this fight,
I will be there by tomorrow night."
Quick reached for his gun, shining and bright,
That had served him in many a fight.

Bright's dreaded disease he long had bore,
And would have fallen to the floor
Had not his queen caught him in her arms,
With loving words with which woman charms
Gently bore him to his bear skin bed.

"My dear Chipeta," he faintly said,
"A message from Ouray you must take,
To Colorow before it is too late,
Tell him not another gun to fire,
Or the Utes will meet with vengeance dire!"
"To serve thee, Ouray, I'd ride through fire,
Thy wish is ever my great desire."

With the proud step of her graceful race,
See her move, quickly from place to place,
Now she stands attired in humble pride,
In all the wild grandeur of her tribe,
"I'll go, brave chief, I am ready now."
Placed her red lips to his noble brow.

Like a fawn into the dark, she ran,
Her eager cry was "Sultan! Sultan!"
A chestnut horse with flowing mane
That well loved her call, swift to her came.
Quickly she bridled and saddled him,
That mountain horse, fleet of hoof and limb,
Then, she lightly to the saddle sprung,
From which the horn of Shavano hung.

Oh I wish you could have seen her there,
To her waist hung braids of long black hair,
Her slender form was a sculptor's dream,
Her soft dreamy eyes, a poet's theme,

Alone, brave, ready to make the ride,
To that land where raged the battle tide,
Her dark eyes raised to the sky to pray,
The good Lord to guide her on the way.

Women who walk in city's bright light,
On that dark night would have died of fright,
Not so, this our heroine of the west,
For with courage grand she was possessed,
She slacked her reins, Sultan bounded to the trail,
That once led down Uncompahgre's vale,
Along the gliding shining river,
Born in the land of gold and silver.

Now she rides where naught but cactus grow,
A sound she hears, 'tis a river's flow,
Gunnison's waters before them roar,
They must swim to reach the farther shore,
Now rides where deep, swift, wild waters wave,
Her hand is the helm, his limb the oar,
A boat they glide to the other shore.

She leaps from horse to give him rest,
For thirty miles he has done his best,
Precious is her time, she must not wait,
On, on, she rides at a rapid gait,
Through lands, then in a wild desert state,
Now the sweet homes of a people great,
Where Eckert and Cedaredge now stand,
Then up they rush to the higher land.

The horse brave of heart, and fleet of limb,
Still flies on a mountain crest to win,
See him climb to high Grand Mesa's rim,
And on its top they stop to view now,
Leon Lake's waters, deep, dark and blue,
The stars above reflected there,
Are a wondrous sight her soul to stir,
Enthralled as a poet in a dream,
Her dark eyes are fixed upon the scene —
Its wondrous beauty fills her soul,
But on she must ride to reach her goal.

Sultan gallops down a winding stream,
That flows through primeval forest green,
To where Colorado's waters flow,
Which are children of their mother snow,
From that river bank so high and steep,
They into the seething waters leap,
And they swim across those waters wide,
And land safely on the other side.

Rider and horse are feeling the strain
Of that ride over mountain and plain,
The saddle she takes from her tired steed,
And turns him loose on the grass to feed —
Forty more miles she must ride today
And finish the trip without delay.

In five hours she gallops over the space,
A terrible sight she now does face:
Chief Douglas, a fair young girl has bound,
Is dragging her over the rough ground,

Up the hill to his gray deer skin tent,
Hill and valley with her shrieks are rent,
A rider and horse fly to her side,
And the brave western heroine cried —

"This sweet girl now is one of our tribe,
For I do adopt her as my child,
She and all these women are now free,
And home I will take the four with me."

Three loud blasts from her horn she then blew,
Which startled hills, vales and mountains too,
A minute more, Colorow and his band,
Of four hundred painted warriors stand,
Around their lovely queen brave and grand,
All these watch the movement of her hand,
With which she gives Ouray's last command.

Silent and still these dark warriors proud,
Vanish from sight as a passing cloud,
And never again their shouts will fill,
With echoes, mountain valley or hill.
Then into the canon she took her way,
Where piles of dead men and horses lay,
A blast from her horn, sounds loud and clear,
Is heard by brave Payne, the pioneer.
He and his men climb over the dead
Behind which for days they've fought and bled —
Beheld the Ute queen lovely and brave,
Who had ridden far, their lives to save.

From their breast burst forth a mighty cheer,
That swept through the canon far and near,
For that woman of a savage race,
Whose history has the proudest place,
Among heroines whose names are placed
Upon the enduring scroll of fame.

Of all her heroic deeds the grandest
Was to give up the home she possessed,
When the Utes were driven from their land,
A sorrowing, lonely, homeless band.
Then devote to them, her precious life,
Away from dead Ouray, yet his loyal wife.

In a land she never loved, she died,
Neglected, poor, no friend at her side,
When daughters of men of nobles fame,
Who fought with Washington, freedom to gain,
Their souls aglow with patriot fires,
Inherited from their gallant sires,
Erected a tomb near Ouray's shrine,
Where Uncompahgre's bright waters sing,
Then brought her body from Utah's land,
And placed it in that Mausoleum grand,
Where in peaceful sleep it is at rest,
In our own dear land she loved the best.

I tell this tale, as she told it to me,
In the year of eighteen ninety-three.

COWBOY JACK

(anonymous)

As recited by Buck Ramsey

He was just a lonely cowboy
With a heart so brave and true,
And he fell in love with a maiden
With eyes of heaven's own blue.

They learned to love each other
And named their wedding day,
But a quarrel came between them
And Jack he rode away.

He joined a band of cowboys
And tried to forget her name,
But out on the lonely prairie
She waits for him just the same.

One night when work was finished
Just at the close of day,
Someone said "Sing a song, Jack,
Just to pass the time away."

When Jack began his singing
His mind it wandered back,
He sang a song of a maiden
Who waited for her Jack.

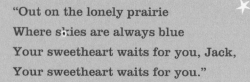

"Out on the lonely prairie
Where skies are always blue
Your sweetheart waits for you, Jack,
Your sweetheart waits for you."

Jack left the camp next morning
Breathing his sweetheart's name,
He said I'll ask forgiveness
For I know that I'm to blame.

But when he reached the prairie
He found a new made mound
His friends they sadly told him
"We've laid your sweetheart down."

They said as she lay dying
She breathed her sweetheart's name,
And asked them with her last breath
To tell him when he came,

"Your sweetheart waits for you, Jack,
Your sweetheart waits for you.
Out on the lonely prairie
Where skies are always blue."

YOUNG CHARLOTTIE
(anonymous)

Young Charlottie lived by a mountain side in a wild and
lonely spot,
There was no village for miles around except her
father's cot;
And yet on many a wintry night young boys would
gather there, —
Her father kept a social board, and she was very fair.

One New Year's Eve as the sun went down, she cast a
wistful eye
Out from the window pane as a merry sleigh went by.
At a village fifteen miles away was to be a ball
that night;
Although the air was piercing cold, her heart was
merry and light.

At last her laughing eye lit up as a well-known voice
she heard,
And dashing in front of the door her lover's sleigh
appeared.
"O daughter, dear," her mother said, "this blanket
'round you fold,
'Tis such a dreadful night abroad and you will catch
your death of cold."

"Oh no, oh no!" young Charlottie cried, as she laughed
like a gipsy queen,
"To ride in blankets muffled up, I never would be seen.
My silken coat is quite enough, you know it is lined
throughout,
And there is my silken scarf to wrap my head and
neck about."

Her bonnet and her gloves were on, she jumped into
    the sleigh,
And swiftly slid down the mountain side and over the
    hills away.
All muffled up so silent, five miles at last were past
When Charlie with few but shivering words, the silence
    broke at last.

"Such a dreadful night I never saw, my reins I can
scarcely hold."
Young Charlottie then feebly said, "I am
    exceedingly cold."
He cracked his whip and urged his speed much faster
    than before,
While at least five other miles in silence had passed o'er.

Spoke Charles, "How fast the freezing ice is gathering
    on my brow!"
Young Charlottie then feebly said, "I'm growing
    warmer now."
So on they sped through the frosty air and the
    glittering cold starlight
Until at last the village lights and the ball-room came
    in sight.

They reached the door and Charles sprang out and
    reached his hands to her.
"Why sit you there like a monument that has no
    power to stir?"
He called her once, he called her twice, she answered
    not a word,
And then he called her once again but still she
    never stirred.

He took her hand in his; 'twas cold and hard as
    any stone.
He tore the mantle from her face while cold stars
    on it shone.
Then quickly to the lighted hall her lifeless form
    he bore; —
Young Charlottie's eyes were closed forever, her voice
    was heard no more.

And there he sat down by her side while bitter tears
    did flow,
And cried, "My own, my charming bride, you
    nevermore shall know."
He twined his arms around her neck and kissed her
    marble brow,
And his thoughts flew back to where she said, "I'm
    growing warmer now."

He took her back into the sleigh and quickly
    hurried home;
When he arrived at her father's door, oh, how her
    friends did mourn;
They mourned the loss of a daughter dear, while
    Charles wept over the gloom,
Till at last he died with the bitter grief, — now they
    both lie in one tomb.

MARTA OF MILRONE

Herman Scheffauer

I shot him where the Rio flows;
I shot him when the moon arose;
And where he lies the vulture knows
Along the Tinto River.

In schools of eastern culture pale
My cloistered flesh began to fail;
They bore me where the deserts quail
To winds from out the sun.

I looked upon the land and sky,
Nor hoped to live nor feared to die;
And from my hollow breast a sigh
Fell o'er the burning waste.

But strong I grew and tall I grew;
I drank the region's balm and dew, —
It made me lithe in limb and thew, —
How swift I rode and ran!

And oft it was my joy to ride
Over the sand-blown ocean wide
While, ever smiling at my side,
Rode Marta of Milrone.

A flood of horned heads before,
The trampled thunder, smoke and roar,
Of full four thousand hoofs, or more —
A cloud, a sea, a storm!

Oh, wonderful the desert gleamed,
As, man and maid, we spoke and dreamed
Of love in life, till white wastes seemed
Like plains of paradise.

Her eyes with Love's great magic shone.
"Be mine, O Marta of Milrone, —
Your hand, your heart be all my own!"
Her lips made sweet response.

"I love you, yes; for you are he
Who from the East should come to me —
And I have waited long!" Oh, we
Were happy as the sun.

There came upon a hopeless quest,
With hell and hatred in his breast,
A stranger, who his love confessed
To Marta long in vain.

To me she spoke: "Chosen mate,
His eyes are terrible with fate, —
I fear his love, I fear his hate, —
I fear some looming ill!"

Then to the church we twain did ride,
I kissed her as she rode beside.
How fair — how passing fair my bride
With gold combs in her hair!

Before the Spanish priest we stood
Of San Gregorio's brotherhood —
A shot rang out! — and in her blood
My dark-eyed darling lay.

O God! I carried her beside
The Virgin's altar where she cried, —
Smiling upon me ere she died, —
"Adieu, my love, adieu!"

I knelt before St. Mary's shrine
And held my dead one's hand in mine,
"Vengeance," I cried, "O Lord, be thine,
But I thy minister!"

I kissed her thrice and sealed my vow, —
Her eyes, her sea-cold lips and brow, —
"Farewell, my heart is dying now,
O Marta of Milrone!"

Then swift upon my steed I lept;
My streaming eyes the desert swept;
I saw the accursed where he crept
Against the blood-red sun.

I galloped straight upon his track,
And never more my eyes looked back;
The world was barred with red and black;
My heart was flaming coal

Through the delirious twilight dim
And the black night I followed him;
Hills did we cross and rivers swim, —
My fleet foot horse and I.

The morn burst red, a gory wound,
O'er iron hills and savage ground;
And there was never another sound
Save beat of horses' hoofs.

Unto the murderer's ear they said,
"Thou'rt of the dead! Thou'rt of the dead!"
Still on his stallion black he sped
While death spurred on behind.

Fiery dust from the blasted plain
Burnt like lava in every vein;
But I rode on with steady rein
Though the fierce sand-devils spun.

Then to a sullen land we came,
Whose earth was brass, whose sky was flame;
I made it balm with her blessed name
In the land of Mexico.

With gasp and groan my poor horse fell, —
Last of all things that loved me well!
I turned my head — a smoking shell
Veiled me his dying throes.

But fast on vengeful foot was I;
His steed fell, too, and was left to die;
He fled where a river's channel dry
Made way to the rolling stream.

Red as my rage the huge sun sank.
My foe bent low on the river's bank
And deep of the kindly flood he drank
While the giant stars broke forth.

Then face to face and man to man
I fought him where the river ran,
While the trembling palm held up its fan
And the emerald serpents lay.

The mad, remorseless bullets broke
From tongues of flame in the sulphur smoke;
The air was rent till the desert spoke
To the echoing hills afar.

Hot from his lips the curses burst;
He fell! The sands were slaked of thirst;
A stream in the stream ran dark at first,
And the stones grew red as hearts.

I shot him where the Rio flows;
I shot him when the moon arose;
And where he lies the vulture knows
Along the Tinto River.

But where she lies to none is known
Save to my poor heart and a lonely stone
On which I sit and weep alone
Where the cactus stars are white.

Where I shall lie, no man can say;
The flowers all arc fallen away;
The desert is so drear and grey,
O Marta of Milrone!

"SUFFRAGE" IN SAGEBRUSH

E.A. Brininstool

She came in by stage from Cayuse; she was young
    and fair to see,
And she had a bunch o' baggage and an air
    o' mystery.
Ev'rybody was a-wonderin' what her graft could
    be, until
Her hull reckerd was made public by ol' one-eyed
    Poker Bill.

She was out for woman suffrage, and it wasn't
    very long
Till she had ol' Sagebrush locoed by the flossy talk
    she slung;
But the Two-Bar foreman cussed her till it must
    hev burned her ears,
'Cuz he couldn't git a puncher to help load a
    car of steers.

Why, she had them Two-Bar punchers all a-taggin'
    at her skirts,
Wearin' "Votes fir Wimmen" ribbons on their faded
    ol' blue shirts!
Ev'ry feller was a boostin' for her doctrine good
    an' hard,
And the cow game was neglected; it was simply
    awful, pard!

She was holdin' daily meetin's over Pinto
    Pete's saloon,
And the Two-Bar bunch attended in a body
    ev'ry noon;
And the way she shot it to 'em — well, it wasn't
    long, you bet,
Till it would hev meant a-killin' to hev knocked the
    suffragette!

The fever got to spreadin' till the Diamond
    Circle crew
Heard her give a talk one mornin' and that outfit
    caught it, too.
And there wasn't a cowpuncher on the range
    for forty mile
But was hot for woman suffrage — and the
    stranger woman's smile.

There's no knowin' how 'twould've ended if she'd
    not eloped one day
With the Two-Bar's night hawss-wrangler,
    although why, she didn't say;
But the foreman jaws and cusses in a way to beat
    the band
When he sights a female stranger gittin' off the
    Overland!

Sweet Betsy from Pike

(anonymous)

A California Immigrant Song of the 1850s

Oh, don't you remember sweet Betsy from Pike
Who crossed the big mountains with her lover Ike,
And two yoke of cattle, a large yellow dog,
A tall, shanghai rooster, and one spotted dog?

Saying, good-bye, Pike County,
Farewell for a while;
We'll come back again
When we've panned out our pile.

One evening quite early they camped on the Platte,
'Twas near by the road on a green shady flat;
Where Betsy, quite tired, lay down to repose,
While with wonder Ike gazed on his Pike County rose.

They soon reached the desert, where Betsy gave out,
And down in the sand she lay rolling about;
While Ike in great terror looked on in surprise,
Saying "Betsy, get up, you'll get sand in your eyes."

Saying, good-bye, Pike County,
Farewell for a while;
I'd go back to-night
If it was but a mile.

Sweet Betsy got up in a great deal of pain
And declared she'd go back to Pike County again;
Then Ike heaved a sigh and they fondly embraced,
And she traveled along with his arm around her waist.

The wagon tipped over with a terrible crash,
And out on the prairie rolled all sorts of trash;
A few little baby clothes done up with care
Looked rather suspicious, — though 'twas all on the square.

The shanghai ran off and the cattle all died,
The last piece of bacon that morning was fried;
Poor Ike got discouraged, and Betsy got mad,
The dog wagged his tail and looked wonderfully sad.

One morning they climbed up a very high hill,
And with wonder looked down into old Placerville;
Ike shouted and said, as he cast his eyes down,
"Sweet Betsy, my darling, we've got to Hangtown."

Long Ike and sweet Betsy attended a dance,
Where Ike wore a pair of his Pike County pants;
Sweet Betsy was covered with ribbons and rings.
Quoth Ike, "You're an angel, but where are your wings?"

THE TRANSFORMATION OF A TEXAS GIRL

James Barton Adams

She was a Texas maiden, she came of low degree,
Her clothes were worn and faded, her feet from shoes
    were free;
Her face was tanned and freckled, her hair was sun-
    burned, too,
Her whole darned tout ensemble was painful for to view!
She drove a lop-eared mule team attached unto a plow,
The trickling perspiration exuding from her brow;
And often she lamented her cruel, cruel fate,
As but a po' white's daughter down in the Lone
    Star State.

No courtiers came to woo her, she never had a beau,
Her misfit face precluded such things as that,
    you know, —
She was nobody's darling, no feller's solid girl,
And poets never called her an uncut Texas pearl.
Her only two companions was those two flea-bit mules,
And these she but regarded as animated tools
To plod along the furrows in patience up and down
And pull the ancient wagon when pap'd go to town.

No fires of wild ambition were flaming in her soul,
Her eyes with tender passion she'd never upward roll;
The wondrous world she'd heard of, to her was
    but a dream

As walked she in the furrows behind that lop-
    eared team.
Born on that small plantation, 'twas there she thought
    she'd die;
She never longed for pinions, that she might rise and fly
To other lands far distant, where breezes fresh and cool
Would never shake and tremble from brayings of
    a mule.

. . . .

But yesterday we saw her dressed up in gorgeous style!
A half a dozen fellows were basking in her smile!
She'd jewels on her fingers, and jewels in her ears —
Great sparkling, flashing brilliants that hung as
    frozen tears!
The feet once nude and soil-stained were clad in
    Frenchy boots,
The once tanned face bore tintings of miscellaneous
    fruits;
The voice that once admonished the mules to move along
Was tuned to new-born music, as sweet as Siren's song!

Her tall and lanky father, one knows as "Sleepy Jim,"
Is now addressed as Colonel by men who honor him;
And youths in finest raiment now take him by the paw,
Each in the hope that some day he'll call him dad-in-law.
Their days of toil are over, their sun has risen at last,
A gold-embroidered curtain now hides their rocky past;
For was it not discovered their little patch of soil
Had rested there for ages above a flow of oil?

CALIFORNIA JOE
(anonymous)

Well, mates, I don't like stories;
Or am I going to act
A part around the campfire
That ain't a truthful fact?
So fill your pipes and listen,
I'll tell you — let me see —
I think it was in fifty,
From that till sixty-three.

You've all heard tell of Bridger;
I used to run with Jim,
And many a hard day's scouting
I've done longside of him.
Well, once near old Fort Reno,
A trapper used to dwell;
We called him old Pap Reynolds,
The scouts all knew him well.

One night in the spring of fifty
We camped on Powder River,
And killed a calf of buffalo
And cooked a slice of liver.
While eating, quite contented,
I heard three shots or four;
Put out the fire and listened, —
We heard a dozen more.

We knew that old man Reynolds
Had moved his traps up here;
So picking up our rifles

And fixing on our gear
We moved as quick as lightning,
To save was our desire.
Too late, the painted heathens
Had set the house on fire.

We hitched our horses quickly
And waded up the stream;
While down close beside the waters
I heard a muffled scream.
And there among the bushes
A little girl did lie.
I picked her up and whispered,
"I'll save you or I'll die."

Lord, what a ride! Old Bridger
Had covered my retreat;
Sometimes that child would whisper
In voice low and sweet,
"Poor Papa, God will take him
To Mama up above;
There is no one left to love me,
There is no one left to love."

The little one was thirteen
And I was twenty-two;
I says, "I'll be your father
And love you just as true."
She nestled to my bosom,
Her hazel eyes so bright,
Looked up and made me happy, —
The close pursuit that night.

One month had passed and Maggie,
We called her Hazel Eye,
In truth was going to leave me,
Was going to say good-bye.
Her uncle, Mad Jack Reynolds,
Reported long since dead,
Had come to claim my angel,
His brother's child, he said.

What could I say? We parted,
Mad Jack was growing old;
I handed him a bank note
And all I had in gold.
They rode away at sunrise,
I went a mile or two,
And parting says, "We will meet again;
May God watch over you."

. . . .

By a laughing, dancing brook
A little cabin stood,
And weary with a long day's scout,
I spied it in the wood.
The pretty valley stretched beyond,
The mountains towered above,
And near its willow banks I heard
The cooing of a dove.

'Twas one grand pleasure;
The brook was plainly seen,
Like a long thread of silver

In a cloth of lovely green;
The laughter of the water,
The cooing of the dove,
Was like some painted picture,
Some well-told tale of love.

While drinking in the country
And resting in the saddle,
I heard a gentle rippling
Like the dipping of a paddle,
And turning to the water,
A strange sight met my view, —
A lady with her rifle
In a little bark canoe.

She stood up in the center,
With her rifle to her eye;
I thought just for a second
My time had come to die.
I doffed my hat and told her,
If it was just the same,
To drop her little shooter,
For I was not her game.

She dropped the deadly weapon
And leaped from the canoe.
Says she, "I beg your pardon;
I thought you was a Sioux.
Your long hair and your buckskin
Looked warrior-like and rough;
My bead was spoiled by sunshine,
Or I'd have killed you sure enough."

"Perhaps it would've been better
If you'd dropped me then," says I;
"For surely such an angel
Would bear me to the sky."
She blushingly dropped her eyelids,
Her cheeks were crimson red;
One half-shy glance she gave me
And then hung down her head.

I took her little hand in mine;
She wondered what it meant,
And yet she drew it not away,
But rather seemed content.
We sat upon the mossy bank,
Her eyes began to fill;
The brook was rippling at our feet,
The dove was cooing still.

'Tis strong arms were thrown around her.
"I'll save you or I'll die."
I clasped her to my bosom,
My long lost Hazel Eye.
The rapture of that moment
Was almost heaven to me;
I kissed her 'mid the tear-drops,
Her merriment and glee.

Her heart near mine was beating
When sobbingly she said,
"My dear, my brave preserver,
They told me you were dead.
But oh, those parting words, Joe,
Have never left my mind,
You said, 'We'll meet again, Mag,'
Then rode off like the wind.

"And oh, how I have prayed, Joe,
For you who saved my life,
That God would send an angel
To guide you through all strife.
The one who claimed me from you,
My Uncle, good and true,
Is sick in yonder cabin;
Has talked so much of you.

"'If Joe were living, darlin,'
He said to me last night,
'He would care for you, Maggie,
When God puts out my light.'"
We found the old man sleeping.
"Hush, Maggie, let him rest."
The sun was slowly setting
In the far-off, glowing West.

And though we talked in whispers
He opened wide his eyes:
"A dream, a dream," he murmured,
"Alas, a dream of lies."
She drifted like a shadow
To where the old man lay.
"You had a dream, dear Uncle,
Another dream to-day?"

"Oh yes, I saw an angel
As pure as mountain snow,
And near her at my bedside
Stood California Joe."
"I'm sure I'm not an angel,
Dear Uncle, that you know;
These hands that hold your hand, too,
My face is not like snow.

"Now listen while I tell you,
For I have news to cheer;
Hazel Eye is happy,
For Joe is truly here."
It was but a few days after
The old man said to me,
"Joe, boy, she is an angel,
And good as angels be.

"For three long months she hunted,
And trapped and nursed me too;
God bless you, boy, I believe it,
She's safe along with you."
The sun was slowly sinking,
When Maggie, my wife, and I
Went riding through the valley,
The tear-drops in her eye.

. . . .

"One year ago to-day, Joe,
I saw the mossy grave;
We laid him neath the daisies,
My Uncle, good and brave."
And comrade, every springtime
Is sure to find me there;
There is something in the valley
That is always fresh and fair.

Our love is always kindled
While sitting by the stream,
Where two hearts were united
In love's sweet happy dream.

Chapter 5

WORDS OF LOVE
FROM THE NEW WEST

 aybe they write their poems on computers and have indoor jobs to supplement their incomes. Still, contemporary cowboys and cowgirls are as sentimental and romantic as their forefathers and just as deeply rooted in American ranch traditions. However, today's poets, often writing without rhyme and meter, are much more direct and explicit in their approach to the mating ritual.

SPARKS
J.B. Allen

YOU RECKON WHY THE WOMEN FOLKS
ALL TRY TO CHANGE THEIR MAN?
THEY LIKED 'IM WELL ENUFF, AT FIRST,
TO TAKE A WEDDIN BAND.

YOU DON'T SUPPOSE, THEY MITE UV BEEN
A PLOTTIN ALL ALONG,
TO STRAIGHTEN UP HIS BATCHIN WAYS,
AND TELL 'IM WHERE HE'S WRONG?

I RECKON THAT IT DON'T HURT MUCH,
TO CIVILIZE A LITTLE,
AND FIND SOME OTHER PLACE TO SIT,
WHILE TAKIN TIME TO WHITTLE.

BUT, IF A FELLER CHANGES,
TILL HE'S NOT THE SAME OL GUY,
THEY MITE BEGIN TO WONDER,
IF IT ALL WAS WORTH THE TRY.

SOMETIMES, IT'S BEST TO LEARN TO LIVE,
WITH EACH ONE'S QUIRKS AND WAYS,
TO KEEP SOME PEACE AND HARMONY,
THRU OUT YOUR MARRIED DAYS.

THEY KEEP THE POT A BOILIN',
TILL THE STEW IS FAIRLY DONE,
FOR, IF THE EMBERS COOL DOWN MUCH,
THERE LIKELY WON'T BE NONE.

A FELLER, I WAS TALKIN TO,
WAS FUSSIN, CAUSE HIS WIFE,
HAD MADE 'IM QUIT A TRUCKIN,
FOR TO LEAD A SETTLED LIFE,
BUT, JUST THE WAY HE TALKED,
AND BUMPED THE CHUTE, TO HELP HIS
FRIEND,
SHORE MADE ME THINK
SHE'D LIKELY COME TO RUE IT,
IN THE END.

FOR THO HE MITE BE HOME EACH NITE,
HIS MIND WILL LIKELY BE,
A SITTIN IN THAT CATTLE TRUCK,
OUT ON THE CONCRETE SEA.

THE SPARKS THAT KEEP A MARRIAGE WARM,
AND HAPPY, THRU THE DAYS,
CAN SHORE GIT SMOTHERED MITY QUICK,
BY CHANGIN PARTNER'S WAYS.

MATRIMONIAL MARTYRS
J.B. Allen

THE WOMEN FOLK,
WHO CAME TO LIVE WITH "MONROE",
EVER YEAR,
JUST COULDN'T STAND THE HARNESS,
FOR THEY, SOON,
WOULD DISAPPEAR.

IT WEREN'T THAT HE WAS MEAN,
OR GAVE 'EM, TROUBLE,
THRU IT ALL,
BUT ONLY,
THAT HIS BATCHIN WAYS,
SOON, STILLED THE MATING CALL!!

THE LIFE,
AROUND THEM DUGOUTS,
OR A LONESOME BOUNDRY SHACK,
HAD NOT,
PREPARED OL "MONROE",
FOR THE MATRIMONY TRACK.

HIS LINE OF TALK,
AROUND IN TOWN,
AND MANNERS,
WERE THE BEST,
BUT, ONE SMALL DOSE,
OF DOUBLE HITCH,
SHORE FAILED,
TO PASS THE TEST.

BUT, STILL,
HE KEPT A TRYIN,
AS, EACH AUTUMN,
BROUGHT ANEW,
SOME FRESH NEW FACE,
TO GRACE THE CAMP,
AND, SEE THE WINTER, THRU.

EACH "BREAKUP",
FOUND 'EM,
BACK IN TOWN,
SOME WISER,
FOR THE TREK.
INCLINED TO PAY,
MOST ANYONE,
TO WRING HIS SCRAWNY NECK!!!

TIMOTHY DRAW
Sue Wallis

We pause at the top of Timothy Draw
Look down the country for stray cows
He cocks his head
Stands in the stirrups
Hands on the horn
Relaxed and easy and graceful
He moves with a horse
Like few men can

In one brief, quick space
I love him more
Than I will ever love again

Like passion, but not of sex
Like Life without death
Like the nudge and the tug and the sleepy smile
Of a too-full child at your still-full breast
Something that explodes from your toes
But flows through your bones
Like warm honey

More powerful than violence

Much Too

. . . Good

To speak of

THE END

Scott S. McKendrick

She was not just a rancher's daughter
With a personality so fine.
How could I ever convince this girl
That I wanted her to be mine?

I'd ask her out and I'd be late,
While waiting she would pine.
How could I ever convince this girl
That I wanted her to be mine?

It pleased me so, the things we'd do
Together from time to time.
How could I ever convince this girl
That I wanted her to be mine?

She could cook, and she could sew;
She could ride a horse so fine.
How could I ever convince this girl
That I wanted her to be mine?

Now time went on, I stood the test
And soon I saw a sign.
How could I ever convince this girl
That I wanted her to be mine?

As we knelt down at the altar,
The music so sublime;
I knew I'd finally convinced this girl
That I wanted her to be mine.

DON'T TEACH THAT GIRL TO ROPE

Scott S. McKendrick

The first mistake I ever made,
Or the first that I'd admit,
Is to teach my girl friend how to rope,
She should have learned to knit.
I thought that it would be so fine,
If my header was my girl.
But now to think of the mess I made,
Would make my straight hair curl.

We practiced long and practiced hard,
As she tried to rope that steer.
I taught her how to swing the rope
Pull the slack, but oh my dear.
"You've got to rope the other end,"
As she let her first loop sail
Pulling hard on the rope,
She had caught the critter's tail.

Well patience must have been with me,
Cuzz I didn't lose my head.
And when she asked, what she'd done wrong,
"Throw farther" was all I said.
Some time went by and then one day,
I could see that she'd improved.
She roped that steer around both horns.
Her skill she finally proved.

We entered shows throughout the West,
We entered as a team.
And when we took the pay check home,
She'd smile at me and beam.
But changes started taking place,
Oh no! how could this be?
She changed her aim from the horns again,
And slipped a loop on me.

THIRTY NINE

Laurie Wagner Buyer

Thirty nine, Dawn beckons me out
into a rose and mauve tumbled sky
adrift with wind-whipped clouds.

Elk squeal, sheltered by willows,
too far away for sight. A night
heron squawks in flight going west.

Twin doe deer pause at the corner
of the yard fence, waiting for me
to choose my daily hiking path.

I turn east, they turn away, toward
the trees, eyes wide, steps soft
and silent, leaving a dew damp trail.

At breakfast, I can't help but smile,
wrapped presents and cards, the fun
of another year just beginning.

All day though, I ponder the most
welcome gifts of all, the gifts
you gave to me before the day —

a sleep-soft kiss, the warm secure
circle of your arms, the privilege
of being your friend, your wife

in this simple life, this world of
willow and river, grass and sky,
and kindred spirit deer walking by.

SEGO LILY

Laurie Wagner Buyer

Cowboy, the world turns too fast anymore.

Firelight brightens your bowed head and clasped
hands that others may mistake for prayer
or contemplation.

Only I know it's longing, loneliness that weights
you so.

High in the hills the horses' night bells ring peace.

But always, the return: the steep rock and sage
covered slopes down to the valley, the weary
ways of those who don't know the meaning of
a sure-footed mule, a sand-bottomed creek, or
a flat, grassy place to unroll a bed.

You know I know. Our descent is difficult.

No words pass between us but in one dancelike
movement
you dismount and take from the sandy soil

a sego lily

trumpet-shaped and fragile, three white petals

tell me how pure the wanting is.

COWBOY DRIFTER
Henry Real Bird

The most beautiful woman, I ever did see
Greets me each mornin', with the star that's light
Spirit of the ground, feelin' of life
In love with a woman
The best I've known
How love has grown
Beyond the stars
With a heart that's good
In your eye, I stood
Way past reflection shadows alive
Cruisin' thru my soul feelin' alive
It damn sure seems like walkin' back
From a good bronc ride walkin' on air
To feel no pain walk on air
To feel no pain walk on air

Cowboy drifter ridin' thru the pines
Up on the head of Custer Creek
Drop off into Reno
Down Medicine Tail
I'm going home I'm going home
To the grass that's blue on the Little Horn
To the grass that's blue on the Little Horn

The most beautiful feelin' I ever did use
Got me this feelin' that I want to live
Just in your arms from here on out
Got me this dream that I want to be
The dream in your heart from here on out
In the little wind after the rain
Sweet smell of sage in the air
Wind inside, on hills that are high
Rivers tip among am I
This is the place where fantasy blends in
       reality
And the sky and ground are one
Reflectin' love I'm ridin' gone
You never did lead me on
Reflectin' love I'm ridin' gone
You never did lead me on

Cowboy drifter ridin' thru the pines
Up on the head of Custer Creek
Drop off into Reno
Down Medicine Tail
I'm going home I'm going home
To the grass that's blue on the Little Horn
To the grass that's blue on the Little Horn

LONE STAR WOMAN

Henry Real Bird

Twas half moon out, on the longest day
Twas rodeoin' about Oklahoma way
Walked in a feeling late at night
Took me a chance turned out right
A Lone Star woman held me tight
She talked of love how it ought to be
Love in thought and just be free
That's what she said, said to me
Feeling love and feeling free
Feeling free and feeling love

A Lone Star Woman whispered love
Took it away before the dawn
A Lone Star Woman in my mind
A Lone Star Woman back in time
Dreamin' of a feelin', in a dream
A Lone Star Woman back in time

Driving down wind river
I'm rodeo bound, long road to hoe
With Lone Star Woman back in mind
All I can do is think of her
Back in time when she was mine
She talked of love how to make love grow
You give alot but not enough
Give alot but not enough
That's the way to make love grow
Feelings Flow and love will grow
Love'll grow when feelings flow
Feelings flow and love will grow

A Lone Star Woman whispered love
Took it away before the dawn
A Lone Star Woman in my mind
A Lone Star Woman back in time
Dreamin' of a feelin', in a dream
A Lone Star Woman back in time
A Lone Star Woman whispered love
Took it away before the dawn

LOVE IS A LADY

Henry Real Bird

Wrote this, once, startin' day anew
Snowfall at night, fresh snow in mornin'.
No tracks in front startin' day anew
Never used to tire of thinkin' of you
But I wrote this one mornin' with nothing in sight
Had a lot of 'em
And if I didn't have my pen and paper
I'd have gone crazy for sure.
I've seen some men out at winter camps
The beauty of a simple life
Accompanied by the bitter simmerin' loneliness
That eats away at the heart and soul and mind of man.

Love is a lady
Who comes walkin' through my mind
Make me think maybe
Should've stayed back in time
In life's feelin', left in time
Long-haired, soft-skinned beauty
Lovin' eyes in evenin' skies
Kissed and held cool summer night
To melt and feel so right
Love is a lady
Who comes out just before the dawn
Make me so happy
To be, in feelin' 'em on
Bird whistlin' mornin' breeze
Ground about day
Livin' love the only way.

Livin' love today
Love is a lady
Who left with a feelin'
Nothing to be free
When there's lonely feelin'
Life'll never be the same
Back in love
Plannin' life
Never enough, now my wife
Reached the end of love
Usin' a heart that's good

Feelin' poured out
Left and gone
Empty feelin' all dried out
Just in song
Of where I long
Love is a lady
In the wind
A whistle, with nothing within
A feelin', with nothing within
Thought of where love had been
Feelin' wrong
Love is a lady
Who comes out just before dawn
Make me so happy
To be in feelin' I'm on
Ground about day
Bird whistlin' mornin' breeze
Spit out your love. . .
All out today

First moon aft sun had turned
Winters 3 since I haven't seen
Half moon longest day
Love comes by just one time
Once in a million
To come by again
Lord, if I'd known
What I know now
Wouldn't be an old man
Tellin' no one that'll listen.

It's in their eye
Reflection in eye
You'll know when you're there
Reflection in eye
Union reflections
Tell of affections
Writin' image of love
My dream
Is to be the dream
Within you
Sounds like
Dreamin' of a feelin'
In a dream
Half moon aft sun had turned
Winters 3 since I haven't seen
Half moon longest day
Love comes by just one time

Once in a million
To come by again
Lord, if I'd known

What I know now
Wouldn't be an old man
Tellin' no one that'll listen.

When you leave
Don't leave nothing behind
Thinkin' you'll be back
You'll never be back
Lookin' for a feelin'
Feelin' empty alone
Out at an old campsite
Wonderin' where flame was
Fire goin' when everything is gone
Feelin' left behind
Will always stay
Lookin' for a feelin'
First moon aft sun had turned
Winters 3 since I haven't seen

Half moon longest day
Love comes by just one time
Once in a million
To come by again
Lord, if I'd known
What I know now
Wouldn't be an old man
Tellin' no one that'll listen
That love comes by? just one time
Once in a million
For love to come by again.

ROSIE'S EAGLE

J.W. Beeson

Rosie was a widow
Who lived up north of town.
If you cross Wolf Creek about a mile
And circle back around,
You'd find a big ol' ranch house
Made from sandstone, rock and sweat
And Rosie raised her family there
Her grandson lives there yet.

Now, I became acquainted
With this grand ol' pioneer
When I was just a youngster,
Nearly in my fourteenth year.
I'd go out and feed her cattle
While Rosie went to stay and
Visit with her children
Who had grown and moved away.

And once, while I was feedin'
I saw a wondrous sight,
A big ol' Golden Eagle
Just soarin' like a kite.
So high above the wagon
He would circle all around
Like he was on a search for
Something down there on the ground.

I watched him for a minute,
Hangin' silent in the sky

But the silence soon was broken
By the echo of his cry,
As he screamed his disapproval
Of the place I chose to rest,
Then I spotted the remainder
Of what once had been a nest.

The nest was old and brittle,
The aftermath of age,
And it layed beside a marker
Nearly covered by the sage.
My youthful curiosity
Had grabbed me by the shirt,
I knew that I had work to do
But five minutes wouldn't hurt.
So I got down off the wagon,
Kicked the tumbleweeds away
Revealing an inscription
In a stone of granite grey.

"Return to me in Springtime with love
        forever new
And dance with me upon the wind, the way
        the eagles do."
I stood there kind a puzzled
Tryin' hard to figure out
Just what these words engraved in stone
Were really all about.
So, when Rose returned from visitin',
I told her what I'd seen
And how when I got near the stone
That bird would start to scream.

With eyes reflecting memories
Through the traces of a tear,
She took me by the hand and said,
"There's something you should hear.
I'll share with you a secret
That up till now's been known
By only me and God above
Of the eagle and the stone.

"The Caliche Hills that weave their way
Through what once was Box-T range
Was once was the home of eagles
That nested on the plains.
And the Indians had a legend
That they believe is true,
That for every man who lived out here,
An eagle lived here too.

"And if the eagles nested
When a man would take a wife
Then the spirits of the lovers
Claimed the nesting ground for life.
And when their life was over,
Their spirit would ascend
And gather with the eagles,
To dance upon the wind.

"And that was how it happened,
As if decreed by fate,
For the day that I became a wife
The eagle took a mate.
And as he made for her a nest of
Willow branch and silt,
I was borne across the threshold
Of a ranch house not yet built.

"And so we spent our wedding night
Beneath the prairie moon,
In a Studebaker wagon
In the early part of June.
And as he held me in his arms
And pledged to me his love,
He said, 'If we should ever part,
I swear by God above,
That in Springtime I'll return to you, as
        when our love began,
And with the eagles we will go, and dance
        upon the wind.'

"The year my husband passed away,
The lady-bird was killed.
They're buried side by side,
Beneath the stone upon the hill.
And every year in early June,
I watch the morning sky
And listen for the sound of wings,
Like angels passin' by.

"And when I see that old eagle,
My heart begins to glow
And I think about a promise
Made so many years ago.
The words are carved in granite, our love
        will never end
And my heart goes up to meet him, and we
        dance upon the wind."

LIGHTS OF LARAMIE

Ian Tyson

What in the world's come over me
I never thought I'd see the day
When that ol' rodeo would turn me loose
And I'd be heading home to stay

Chorus:
Now I'm lookin' for the lights of Laramie
I never thought I'd miss you so
If you let me in your lovin' arms in Laramie
I'll never ever let you go
Girl, I'll never ever let you go

Can't leave your memory behind
Don't matter where I go
Don't matter what I do
If God gave Wyoming to the wind
He must have given my heart to you
Forever and ever

Chorus:

Oh how those lights like diamonds shine
Across that wild and windy plain
Ain't nothin' in the world I wouldn't give to be
A diamond in your eyes again
Forever and ever

Chorus:

NAVAJO RUG
Ian Tyson and Tom Russell

Well it's two eggs up on whiskey toast
And home fries on the side
Wash it down with roadhouse coffee
Burns up your insides
Just a Canyon-Colorado Diner
And a waitress I did love
I sat in the back 'neath an old stuffed bear
And a worn out Navajo rug
Now Old Jack the boss he left at six
And it's Katie bar the door
She'd pull down that Navajo rug
And she spread it 'cross the floor
Hey, I saw lightning 'cross the sacred
    mountains
Saw woven turtledoves
I was lying next to Katie
On that old Navajo rug

Chorus:
Aye aye aye Katie
Shades of red and blue
Aye aye aye Katie
Whatever became of the Navajo rug and
    you

Well I saw Old Jack about a year ago
He said the place burned to the ground
And all I saved was this here old bear tooth
And Katie she's left town
But Katie she got her souvenir too
Jack spat a tobacco plug

You should have seen her a-coming through
    the smoke
A-dragging that Navajo rug

Chorus

So every time I cross the sacred mountains
And lightning breaks above
It always takes me back in time
To my long lost Katie love
But everything keeps on a-movin'
And everybody's on the go
You don't find things that last anymore
Like an old woven Navajo

Aye aye aye Katie
Shades of red and blue
Aye aye aye Katie
What ever became of the Navajo rug and
    you Katie
Shades of red and blue

THE POETS

Cowboy poets have always been independent and straightforward, just like the folks who settled the West. Don't assume by their "ain'ts" and dialect and unusual punctuation that their work should be taken any less seriously than that of other American poets. Plenty have fancy diplomas and literary success in other genres. Some — Charles Lummis and Earl A. Brininstool, included — were never even cowboys. Once a buckaroo, the long-revered Bruce Kiskaddon worked as a bell-hop and movie extra in L.A. in his later life. Charles "Badger" Clark spent about six years as a cowboy and then devoted the rest of his life to writing poetry about it. Prolific writer S. Omar Barker was once a legislator as well as a rancher. Yet, the verse they wrote so vividly reflects their knowledge of cowboy life that it is accepted by the cowboy culture as the genuine goods.

The major cowboy contributors are included in these biographies. However, some authors are omitted, especially those with just one poem represented. Wherever there was a name attached to an old poem, we included it, although many were published anonymously. A few poets were really unknown beyond their names attached to a verse submitted to an old western newspaper. For instance, "Chipeta's Ride" was originally submitted to a western journal by a John W. Taylor, who may have been a man born in Ireland who owned a mine at St. Elmo, Colorado. Then again, he could have been someone else. Our apologies, likewise, to Herman Scheffauer, the author of "Marta of Milrone," which appeared in *Songs of the Cattle Trail & Cow Camp,* by John Lomax.

— *The editors*

Anonymous: As far back as the 1840s, cowboys were reciting and singing verses they heard elsewhere. Some poems traveled across the country and over so many years that the author's name was forgotten. And many of the poems published in early newspapers and magazines were unsigned, perhaps due to the humility of the poet.

James Barton **Adams**, one of a few cowboy poets to publish his works before the turn of the century, is best remembered for his robust verse, "The Cowboy's Dance Song," printed here in Chapter Two, "Cowboy Goes A-Courtin'." In addition to his book *Breezy Western Verse* (1889), Adams' work has been included in several collections, including John A. Lomax's *Songs of the Cattle Trail and Cow Camp* (Macmillan Co., 1919).

J.B. **Allen** (born 1953) has been a cowboy for three decades, heading ranches from the Great Divide to Fort Worth, Texas. He draws on this experience, dialect and stories heard from old-timers in writing his poems, most of which are based on actual events. Some of his favorite works appear in his own collection, *Water Gap Wisdom* (1990) and on a later tape, *Kindred Spirits*. Currently he and his wife live in Whiteface, Texas, where Allen has "a few of my own cows stuck together" and works as night foreman on a feed lot.

S. Omar **Barker** (1894-1985) was born and educated in New Mexico at the turn of the century and worked at ranching, teaching, newspaper and magazine writing, publicity and forestry. The often honored writer was born in a log cabin and lived in New Mexico his entire life, publishing many books of verse, including *Vientos de las Sierras* (1924) and *Buckaroo*

Ballads (1928). His poetry, with an emphasis on rhythm and rhyme, is a pleasure to recite and has been swapped around campfires since the 1920s. His last book, *Rawhide Rhymes: Singing Poems of the Old West* (1968) was published by Doubleday & Co.

J.W. **Beeson** (born 1951) is a native Texan who has cowboyed and rodeoed since he was a youngster. He sings as well as writes his own poems and songs. His work has appeared in several publications including *Western Horseman* and *Coolin' Down* (1993), a compilation of contemporary cowboy verse. "Rosie's Eagle" first appeared on his own cassette album, *Last of a Breed* (1991). With 15 years experience in saddlery, he makes a saddle every now and then, recites at cowboy poetry gatherings and does cowboy day work in Shattuck, Oklahoma.

Earl Alonzo **Brininstool** (1870-19?) was a newspaperman and writer, not a working cowboy. But you wouldn't know it from reading *Trail Dust of a Maverick*. First published in 1914, and then expanded in 1921, it's as detailed and vivid an account of the changing West as you'll see in verse, whether it's tongue-in-cheek poetry such as "Love on the Bar X" or the haunting "Juanita." He lived most of his life in Los Angeles, joining a group of western artists including Will Rogers and Charles Russell who met once a month at the University Club. His contributions to the history of the Old West include *The Bozeman Trail* (1922), which he wrote with Dr. Grace Raymond Hebard of the University of Wyoming.

Laurie Wagner **Buyer** (born 1954, in Edinburgh, Scotland) spent her early years hopping the globe with her family before

settling in Illinois. She interrupted her college career to homestead on the North Fork of the Flathead River in Montana
while working part time for the U.S. Geological Survey, but
later was graduated from Montana State University, Bozeman,
in 1980. A real cowgirl, Buyer has worked on ranches in Montana and Wyoming while writing and taking photographs. Her
works have appeared in numerous publications, including
Fence Post and *Dry Crik Review*. Today, she and her husband
run a cow-calf operation on the South Fork of the South Platte
River near Fairplay, Colorado.

Robert V. **Carr** lived around the turn of the 19th century, writing delightfully romantic verses such as "Love Lyrics of a Cowboy" and "A Romance on the Range," as well as the two-stan-
za, untitled verse that begins our book. He contributed verse
to numerous magazines before publishing *Black Hills Ballads*
in Denver, 1902. A second volume, *Cowboy Lyrics*, was pri-
vately published in 1908 and has become a much sought-after
collector's item in the cowboy poetry community. An augment-
ed edition was republished in Los Angeles in 1912. We wish
we knew more of the man who wrote, upon falling in love:
"Can scarcely sleep or eat my chuck — Dog-gone the luck? I
guess I'm stuck."

Charles "Badger" **Clark** (1883-1957), named South Dakota's
first poet laureate in 1937 (an honor he held until his death) is
one of the most recited cowboy poets of this century. His
father, a Methodist minister, helped establish Wesleyan University of Mitchell, South Dakota. His mother, whose maiden
name was Badger, died when he was a boy. His career began
with a poem he sent home to his stepmother while cowboying
from 1906 to 1910 at the Cross I Quarter Circle Ranch in

Tombstone, Arizona. She sent it on to the *Pacific Magazine* which published it and later ran his famed "A Border Affair" in 1907. After four years of cowboying, Clark returned to the Black Hills of South Dakota where he lived out his remaining years on the meager royalties from his poetry and public speaking engagements. He was engaged to the same woman, twice, but never married. "If any woman knew how much money I made, she'd never marry me," he often said.

Frank **Desprez'** "Lasca" is one of the most beautiful love poems to come out of the Western frontier. According to cowboy historians Austin and Alta Fife, it was first published in the *Montana Live-Stock Journal*, June 16, 1888.

Gail I. **Gardner** (1892-1989) is perhaps best remembered for his poem, "Sierry Pete's" (also called "Tying the Knots in the Devil's Tail"). Born in Prescott, Arizona, he graduated from Dartmouth College in 1914 and returned to Prescott to help run his father's general merchandise store until he bought into a cow outfit in Skull Valley, Arizona. In 1917, when he was headed back to Washington, D.C. to get into military service, Gardner penned "Sierry Pete's." Gardner served as Prescott postmaster from 1936 to 1957 and published *Orejana Bull: For Cowboys Only*, his only book of poems, in 1935.

Bruce **Kiskaddon** (1878-1950) was a working cowboy who always had a knack for making up little jingles. Encouraged by one of his bosses, he published a small book of his poems, *Rhymes of the Ranges,* in 1924. After cowboying in Australia, he and friends came to Hollywood on a whim, hoping to land jobs riding horses in movies. After driving a chariot in the original silent version of *Ben Hur* and a few stuntman gigs, he spent the last third of his life as a bellhop in Los Angeles hotels. He married and had one daughter, and knew he couldn't support a family on a cowboy's wage. But he could always return to the life he loved through his poetry, which he wrote between tips and published in *Western Livestock*.

Henry Herbert **Knibbs** (1874-1922) was born in Ontario, Canada, and attended both Ridley College in Ontario and Harvard University before pursuing the cowboy's life for a time in Arizona, New Mexico and California. Although much of his verse was Victorian-style poems, he is best remembered for his finely crafted cowboy poems. Many of these were published in his *Songs of the Trail* (1920); *Saddle Songs* (1922) and *Songs of the Last Frontier* (1930).

Charles F. **Lummis** (1859-1928) was a rough-hewn Renaissance man, a poker-playing, carousing adventurer who left Harvard under a cloud of scandal and married a medical student. He went to work on his father-in-law's farm in Ohio, but found journalism more to his liking. He landed a job as the first city editor of the *Los Angeles Times* by walking from Cincinnati to Los Angeles in 1885 and chronicling his adventures in the *Times*. Lummis' many books, photographs and Native American crafts are at the Southwest Museum in Los Angeles, which he founded in 1907. His book of poetry, *A Bronco Pegasus*, includes still photographs by Lummis. He was never a cowboy. But he loved the West and immersed himself in American Indian as well as Hispanic culture.

Scott S. **McKendrick** (born 1951) is a cowboy humorist and poet born and raised in Tooele, Utah. His father was a horseshoer, trainer and calf roper and McKendrick has spent most of his life on horseback, marrying a female buckaroo from Nevada, Rena Johns. They live, with their three kids, in Trenton, Utah, where the poet has a part-time horseshoeing business and is state 4-H program leader at Utah State University. Contrary to his poetic advice, he did teach his girl to rope. He's teaching his daughters as well.

Waddie **Mitchell** (born 1950), grew up on his father's ranch in Elko and has been a cowboy all of his life. The much lauded poet quickly became the best-known figure on the contemporary western poetry scene when he made his first appearance on the *Johnny Carson Show* in 1985. He won the Governor's Arts Award in Literature for the state of Nevada and was the first inductee to the Cowboy Poets and Singers Hall of Fame. His published works include *Waddie Mitchell's Cowboy Christmas Poems* (Peregrine Smith, 1987) and *Cowboy's Night Before Christmas* (Peregrine Smith, 1993). He has an award-winning video *Buckaroo Bard* (1987), hosted by Richard Farnsworth and produced by BYU Productions. He records his poetry under the Warner Western label; his albums include *Lone Driftin' Rider* (1992) and *Buckaroo Poet* (1993). Mitchell has five children.

Buck **Ramsey** (born 1938), resides in Amarillo, Texas, with his wife Bette and has spent most of his life in that state. He was a cowboy along the Canadian River in the Texas Panhandle for a number of years. He was thrown from a horse and confined to a wheelchair, which led to his own cowboy poetry as well as moving recitations of classics. His epic poem, "And as I Rode Out in the Morning," was published by Texas Tech University Press in 1993. Ramsey has also released a compact disc, *Rolling Up Hill from Texas* (1992). Buck's version of

"Cowboy Jack" was sung without accompaniment, just as it was in the cowboy's oral tradition.

Henry **Real Bird** (born 1948) is a Crow Indian who grew up on the reservation on the Little Big Horn, Montana. Today he runs a ranch on the east end of the reservation, in the Wolf Teeth Mountains and is registrar at Little Big Horn College. The land around his mountains is the inspiration for much of his free verse. His style departs from traditional, rhymed verse, yet his images and subjects are true to the cowboy tradition.

Tom **Russell**, who wrote "Navajo Rug" with Ian Tyson, says he grew up in Southern California in the 1950s. "Navajo Rug" was the country music single of the year in Canada in 1987. He recently received an ASCAP Award for "Outbound Plane," one of the most radio-performed songs of 1992.

Belle **Starr** (1848?-1889) is, according to Jack Thorp, the author of "Bucking Broncho," a poem that appears in Chapter Three, "The Heartbroke Cowboy." She is the famous outlaw glamorized in *Belle Starr, the Bandit Queen* by Richard J. Fox, who rode with Jesse James' gang, the Younger gang and other American outlaws. Her first husband was outlaw Jim Reid. When he died, she married Sam Starr, an Indian, and they moved to Indian Territory in Oklahoma, where she was a frequent hostess to outlaws in retreat.

Ed **Steele** (1913-1988) was a cowboy and mule wrangler at the Grand Canyon in the '30s and '40s, until a foot disease made it impossible for him to walk. He was not known beyond his circle of friends, but his songs, for which he got no credit, were sung and recorded by other cowboy entertainers.

Although they never entered the oral tradition, they are gems of cowboy verse. In 1985, "The Phantom Ranch Dream," was performed at the fiftieth reunion of the original Grand Canyon Cowboy Band in Prescott, Arizona. One of the original band members, John Bradley, reports that "Ed got his last wish": The old cowboy was driven to the graveyard in an open wagon by a team of mules.

N. Howard "Jack" **Thorp** (1867-1940) is one of the most important and earliest chroniclers of cowboy poetry. He traveled 1500 miles on horseback through Texas to New Mexico in 1889 and 1890, collecting verse from cowboys on working cow camps. He self-published his first book, *Songs of the Cowboys* (1908), a little paper-covered volume that included five of his own poems. But he spent most of his years living the cowboy life in New Mexico.

K. **Tolliver**'s "The Rambling Cowboy" has been recited and passed around from cowboy to cowboy since the early 1900s. The poem first appeared in print in John A. Lomax's 1910 edition of *Cowboy Songs and Other Frontier Ballads*.

Ian **Tyson** (born 1934) is both a rancher and acclaimed performing and recording musician. In fact, in 1989 he was inducted into the Canadian Country Music Hall of Honour. Today his ranch is in the foothills of the Rocky Mountains. Once known to many as half of the successful '60s folk duo Ian and Sylvia, Tyson learned to play the guitar while recovering from a rodeo accident. The pair cut more than a dozen albums, including songs such as Tyson's *Four Strong Winds* and *Someday Soon*, and Sylvia Fricker's *You Were on My Mind*. Since 1963, Tyson has owned a farm east of Toronto and has been rodeoing and raising cutting horses. His newest album is *18 Inches of Rain* (Vanguard and Stony Plain Records).

Sue **Wallis** (born 1957) descends from several generations of ranching folk and rodeo people, and grew up a-horseback on the Bittercreek side of the Greenough Ranch amongst cattle people of the old school. She now lives with her children in the shadow of the Ruby Mountains, not far from Deeth, Nevada. Her adventurous career has run the gamut from cowboying to politicking, and everything in between, including roughneck work on uranium explosion rigs. While pursuing a degree in American Studies from the University of Wyoming, she completed two honors theses on the tradition of cowboy poetry. She now works for the Western Folklife Center in Elko, Nevada. She was a consultant on the PBS series, *The United States of Poetry*.

♥

ACKNOWLEDGEMENTS

No anthology of historical cowboy poetry would be complete without verse from the original compilations of cowboy songs: *Songs of the Cowboy* (Estancia, New Mexico: News Print Shop, 1908) by N. Howard "Jack" Thorp, *Cowboy Songs and Other Frontier Ballads* (The Macmillan Company, 1910) and *Songs of the Cattle Trail and Cow Camp* (The Macmillan Company, 1919) by John Avery Lomax. Thorp and Lomax were the pioneers who traveled throughout the West, collecting the songs and poems recited by the American cowboy.

Early poets whose works are represented in this book include E.A. Brininstool (*Trail Dust of a Maverick*, Dodd Mead & Co., 1914), Robert V. Carr (*Cowboy Lyrics*, W.B. Conkey Company, 1908), Henry Herbert Knibbs (*Songs of the Trail*, Houghton Mifflin, 1920) and Charles "Badger" Clark (*Sun and Saddle Leather*, Richard G. Badger, 1915).

We are also indebted to Guy Logsdon, University of Tulsa, author of *Whorehouse Bells are Ringing* (1982), for his generous advice.

Thanks also to F.E. Abernathy of the Texas Folk and Folklore Society, for his guidance and permission to reprint "Tonight My Heart's in Texas." We also thank Bernis Argo, Westerner's International, for information on Charles "Badger" Clark.

Our gratitude to Robert and Jodie Phillips for permission to print the poems of S. Omar Barker. Thanks also to Gail Steiger for permission to reprint his grandfather Gail Gardner's "Cowboy Love Song."

Others to whom we are indebted include Hal Cannon and Sue Wallis of the Western Folklife Center in Elko, Nevada; Carol A. Edison of the Utah Folklife Center; Barbara Walker and Karen Kreiger of the Utah State University Fife Folklore Archive for their research assistance; cowboy poet Buck Ramsey for his recitations and recommendations; John Bradley of Cottonwood, Arizona, for keeping Ed Steele's songs alive; Katie Lee for her numerous suggestions and research materials; John Dofflemeyer, editor of Dry Crik Review, for his early help and direction, and Warren Miller of Sharlot Hall Museum and Jay Dusard, both of Prescott, Arizona.

Our thanks also to Erin Douglas, Melissa Hoffs, Patricia Fox, Robert Cohn, Neil Feineman, Ann Calistro, Gloria List, Rik Krulish, Van-Martin Rowe, Mal Hoffs, Richard A. Penn, Susan DeLand at the Gene Autry Western Heritage Museum, as well as the staff at the UCLA University Research Library Department of Special Collections.

And finally and most certainly, thanks to Tony and Nann Durando and George and Dianne Lange.

♥

CREDITS

"Pony Tracks" and "Old San Antone" by Henry Herbert Knibbs, are from *Songs of the Trail* by Henry Herbert Knibbs. Copyright © 1920 by Henry Herbert Knibbs, © renewed 1948 by Ida Julia Knibbs. Reprinted by permission of Houghton Mifflin Co. All rights reserved.

Poems by S. Omar Barker, including "Jest Bring Me Back My Cowgirl Gal!," "For the Love of Lily," "One Way of Proposin'" and "Lonesome" are reprinted with the permission of Robert Phillips for the estate of S. Omar Barker.

"Tonight My Heart's in Texas," is from the article "Songs the Cowboys Sing" by John R. Craddock, found in Publications of the Texas Folklore Society XXVI, titled *Texas Folk & Folklore*, 1954.

"Timothy Draw" by Sue Wallis was first published in *The Exalted One*, Dry Crik Press, Lemon Cove, CA., 1991.

"Sego Lily" by Laurie Wagner Buyer was previously published in *Dry Crik Review*, Winter '92, Volume II, No. 1.

Jack R. Lamb, a co-editor of this book, has traveled through many western states, gathering poems and interviews and researching the cowboy's oral tradition. He began interviewing cowboy poets in 1989, while studying American literature at the University of California, San Diego. In 1992, he received a fellowship at the university, which resulted in his thesis, "Cowboy Poetry: History and Orality."

INDEX

Poems

Poets

ANGEL CITY PRESS

Angel City Press, Inc. was established in 1992, and is dedicated to the publication of high-quality nonfiction and poetry. Angel City Press is located in Santa Monica, California.

COWBOY LOVE POETRY

Cowboy Love Poetry was designed by Jeff Darnall of Darnall Design, Laguna Niguel, California. The book was produced on an Apple Macintosh IIcx. Programs used include QuarkXPress, Adobe Illustrator and Adobe Photoshop. Fonts used include Clarendon, Serifa Roman and Helvetica. The book was printed on a Harris 77-inch sheet-fed press at the Kingsport, Tennessee, facility of Arcata Graphics Company.